# Finding and H
# In A Week

Nigel Cumberland

Nigel Cumberland has worked in the corporate recruitment field for over 15 years, having previously worked as a Finance Director with Coats plc where he often had to recruit new staff. He has run offices for some of the world's leading recruitment firms: Adecco SA, Hays plc and Harvey Nash plc. In addition he created his own award-winning recruitment firm in Hong Kong and China called St George's which was later sold to Hays plc.

Today Nigel runs a talent and leadership training and coaching consultancy called the Silk Road Partnership. He regularly consults, gives workshops and lectures to organizations on how to optimally attract, recruit and retain talent.

Having worked all over the world for over 25 years, Nigel understands the global and cultural issues of recruitment as well as appreciating the common challenges facing anyone trying to fill a job vacancy – be it in Manchester, Chicago, Shanghai or Cape Town.

He was educated at Cambridge University, is a former chartered accountant (FCMA) and is an accredited executive coach and leadership training professional (Fellow of both the ICPA and of the InstLM).

He currently lives in Dubai with his wife, Evelyn, and son, Zeb.

Teach<sup>®</sup> Yourself

# Finding and Hiring Talent In A Week

Nigel Cumberland

First published in Great Britain in 2012 by Hodder Education.

This edition published in 2016 by John Murray Learning

First published in US in 2016 by Quercus.

Copyright © Nigel Cumberland 2012, 2016

*British Library Cataloguing in Publication Data:* a catalogue record for this title is available from the British Library.

ISBN 9781473623804

eISBN 9781473623828

1

Typeset by Cenveo® Publisher Services.

Printed and bound in Great Britain by CPI Group (UK) Ltd., Croydon, CR0 4YY.

John Murray Learning policy is to use papers that are natural, renewable and recyclable products and made from wood grown in sustainable forests. The logging and manufacturing processes are expected to conform to the environmental regulations of the country of origin.

Carmelite House
50 Victoria Embankment
London EC4 0DZ
www.hodder.co.uk

# Contents

# Introduction

Today, knowledge and human capital are becoming an organization's key resources, and the ability to find, attract and retain talent has become an essential skill that any successful organization must embrace. Likewise, if you wish to become a successful business leader, you must master the skills of talent management, including recruitment. Recruitment skills can only be acquired through practice and this book can act as your guidebook to ensure that you will be as successful as possible with any future recruitment that you undertake.

Many assume that recruitment is an area of business where one must only be very systematic and organized to produce optimal results. This is true and as you read this book you will notice that recruitment will often be referred to as the process of recruitment or as the recruitment process. Likewise, one often talks about recruitment as managing the recruitment pipeline with applicants entering one end of the pipe and successful new employees coming out of the other end.

However, recruitment is also an art and involves developing people and leadership skills that cannot be totally taught. Only through experience can you become a better judge of whether a certain candidate will be the best fit for a particular job role, company culture and management style. In spite of many years of recruitment gurus advising the business world, a surprisingly high proportion of new employees do not succeed with their new employers.

## '50% of American workers quit in the first 6 months'

Leigh Branham, Saratoga Institute

In seven chapters, this book will walk you through the entire recruitment process showing you how to succeed, what pitfalls to not ignore and where to put special attention. These seven chapters will cover:

- How to exactly define your recruitment needs, showing you how to develop and create job descriptions that capture what a job role's tasks and responsibilities are and what the needed characteristics of a candidate are to fill such a role
- Sourcing and finding candidates both locally and further afield through various channels including recruitment firms, jobsites, referrals, job fairs and social networks
- How to attract candidates through having a great employer branding and marketing message or sale pitch
- Successfully interviewing candidates to find out which ones would make excellent employees and also using the interviews as an opportunity to sell the company and the job opportunity to the candidates
- Choosing the ideal candidate through using assessment tools, giving good feedback, background checks, ranking candidates and communicating well with candidates
- How to make sure that your chosen candidate accepts your job offer by getting the candidate 'across the line' and understanding how to give a candidate an offer of employment
- Ensuring that the chosen candidate becomes a successful employee who passes their probation period and has their expectations met, thus ensuring that you can call the recruitment a success

# SUNDAY

# Defining your recruitment needs

> *'I am convinced that nothing we do is more important than hiring and developing people. At the end of the day you bet on people, not on strategies.'*
>
> Larry Bossidy

The entire recruitment process begins with the need for two critical questions: 'What job role are we wishing to fill?' and 'The role needs to be filled by what kind of individual?'

Companies that fail to give these two questions enough thought should not be surprised when they later face difficulties in attracting enough suitable candidates, in agreeing who to hire or in being able to attract a suitable candidate to join them. This chapter will help you to avoid these problems by ensuring that the foundation of your planned recruitment process is clearly thought through and planned.

This chapter will show you how to:

- Define a job role correctly in terms of what the role's tasks, goals, needed skills or competencies are and the type of role (e.g. full-time or part-time role)
- Create an ideal candidate profile including an understanding of the required work experience, educational background and qualifications
- Combine the job role and candidate profile to produce a job description that can later be used in the recruitment process (e.g. to create job adverts and to write interview questions)
- Agree and to gain approval for the recruitment process (this will include discussion about understanding the expected cost and time frame of the entire recruitment process)

# Why do you need to recruit somebody?

This simple question needs to be asked and answered in order to ensure that the entire recruitment process starts and flows well.

The reasons for you needing to recruit may include:

- A person in your organization has been laid off or fired.
- A person has resigned from their position.
- A person has been moved or promoted leaving their position vacant.
- A single new position has been created or possibly a number of new positions are being created (e.g. perhaps a new business line or department is being set up).

Candidates will want to know why there is a vacancy and you must understand that there is a big difference between such answers as:

'This is a new position that we have created.'

'The last person left the company because the position is so demanding and stressful.'

# Creating a job description

A job description is a document that is normally only one or two pages in length, which describes the key aspects of the job that you wish to fill and is made up of:

- the job title and the title of the role it reports to
- the tasks, responsibilities and activities that need to be carried out by the job-holder
- the skills, background, qualifications and experience that are required to perform the job well.

You would be surprised how often companies try to fill vacant positions without any agreed job description or any list of duties and activities that somebody in the role would have to fulfil and carry out. Without having a clear and agreed job

description, it is very difficult to create job advertisements, create interview questions or to be able to give a clear answer to a candidate who asks the following kind of questions:

- 'If I were to work in this role, what would I be expected to do and how would my performance be measured and judged?'
- 'Am I suitably qualified to be able to perform this role well?'

You may be lucky enough to have an existing description of the job's duties and this may only need updating and editing. However, very often you will not be so lucky and you will need to create an entirely new job description. The following sections walk you through how to create such a new job description.

## Job title and reporting line

First, you need to decide on the job title that you wish to give the role. Sometimes this is a very easy task to do, but often there are a number of possible titles from which you need to choose, with some titles being more attractive and enticing to potential candidates than others, perhaps because a certain title sounds more senior or more modern. As an example, which title in each of these pairs of job titles would seem more appealing and attractive?

| | |
|---|---|
| Accounting Supervisor | Accounting Manager |
| Payroll Clerk | Payroll & Remuneration Specialist |
| Recruitment Coordinator | Sourcing Specialist |
| Mechanic | Mechanical Specialist |

Why does the job title matter? You need to market and sell your opportunity, and the more attractive the job title is the greater your chances of having more candidates from which to choose.

It is also good to include details in the job description of the job title that the role will report to, for example the Sales Executive reports to a District Sales Manager or the Accountant reports to the Finance Controller.

## The tasks and responsibilities

Second, you need to write down what the job actually involves doing. This is in terms of the tasks, responsibilities and activities. But is this enough information? I would recommend that you also write down for each task some indications of the level of performance expected or goals and targets to be achieved. Here are a couple of simple examples:

| Task, responsibility or activity | Performance level or goal expected |
|---|---|
| Manage the payroll system | Without any errors; in a timely manner |
| In charge of purchasing office supplies | To keep the spending within budget; maintain all paperwork; obtain three quotations per purchase |

From this information, you can create meaningful and clear descriptions of the job's duties. For the two examples above, the descriptions could be written as follows:

● Managing the company's payroll system ensuring that all transactions are accurate and are carried out in a timely manner

- Tasked with the office supplies procurement process, which includes obtaining vendor quotations, maintaining the procurement files and keeping the expenditure within budgeted levels

## Skills and qualifications required

The final part of a normal job description is to work out what the ideal candidate for the job should possess in terms of education, qualifications, work experience and other skills or competencies.

In creating such a list, it is helpful to think through the following questions:

- What types of skills, experiences and knowledge are really needed to enable someone to perform in the role very well? Which of these are essential traits and which are preferred traits?
- To succeed in your company, what kind of skills, experience and knowledge are really needed? How many of the top performers have or do not have certain skills and qualifications?

Let us explore each part in a little more detail.

### Education

Do you require someone to fill your role who:

- is a school leaver (leaving after GCESs, A-levels or the SAT)?
- has completed a qualification at a college or technical institute?
- has been to university (and obtained a diploma, Bachelors, Masters or a higher degree)?

Be honest in your choice and ask yourself and your colleagues the question: *'Does the job vacancy you are recruiting to fill really need a highly educated candidate?'* Today we normally seek university graduates to fill so many jobs that only 10 or 20 years ago were being comfortably performed by those who had finished their formal studies at 16 or 18 years of age. Remember that not every high-performing person has a university degree, with notable examples including Bill Gates and Richard Branson.

### Professional qualifications

In addition to the school, college and university qualifications, there are many other kinds of qualifications which are given by professional bodies such as the nursing, accounting, executive coaching, human resources, insurance, engineering and medical fields. There are hundreds of such professional bodies at the local, national and international levels.

Such qualifications are normally linked to having to be a member of the relevant association or organization and may include an accreditation.

Are there any qualifications that the job-holder must possess to be able to legally perform the job? Examples might include needing to be a qualified and registered nurse to work as a nurse or care-giver.

Likewise, does a particular job vacancy require certain skills that can only come from having qualified with a particular institute or organization? A common example is needing an accounting qualification to be able to work as an accountant in the accounting and finance profession.

## Work experience, technical (or hard) skills and knowledge

A person's work experience, their acquired skills and knowledge are sometimes used as a measure of whether a person can do the job.

The list of possible required abilities and skills is endless and may include:

- Do they have the ability to operate the computer programme?
- Can they operate the welding equipment?
- Are they able to drive a bus?
- Can they speak French?
- Can they consolidate financial accounts?
- Do they know how to review engineering drawings?

For your role opening, you should ask:

- What does a candidate actually have to be able to do well?
- How many years of work experience are really required?
- Are you seeking actual evidence of the person doing certain tasks and activities? Or are you simply seeking a certain level of maturity which comes with working experience and with age?

I ask this last question because from my many years of recruitment experience I know that very often we over-engineer our job descriptions and we seek a candidate with work experience and skills that in truth are not really necessary to perform the job role well.

## Soft skills and competencies

Soft skills refer to a person's mind-set, attitude, character and personality and are sometimes referred to as competencies or behavioural competencies.

We are all very good at judging people, rightly or wrongly, in this area, making comments such as:

- He is very lazy and not persistent.
- She seems to lack good people skills.
- He is always too aggressive with his staff.

A person's soft skills and competencies can be used to answer the question as to whether somebody will be able to do the job well.

To succeed in the job opening, what kind of soft skills and competencies should a candidate possess?

For the person to fit into your organization and culture, what kind of additional soft skills and competencies may be required?

The following examples of soft skills will help you to determine which are important to look for in candidates you may wish to hire, and which you may need to list in any job descriptions you are writing.

SUNDAY
MONDAY
TUESDAY
WEDNESDAY
THURSDAY
FRIDAY
SATURDAY

- Communication skills
- A sense of humour
- Service mentality
- Problem-solving
- Being open
- Adaptable
- Delegation skills
- Creativity
- Persistence
- Understanding our role and responsibilities
- Team working
- Interpersonal skills
- Able to build relationships
- Time management
- Professionalism
- Accuracy
- Proactive
- Empathy
- Trust
- Patience
- Presentation skills
- Supportive
- Tolerance
- Integrity

Perhaps your organization has already created a structured competency model, in which job roles have been studied and the list of necessary soft skills and competencies required to succeed in each role have been agreed upon and listed.

If not, you must simply try to list the required soft skills and competencies that you determine are needed. Try observing people who are performing in the same or in a similar role – what soft skills do they need to do their job well? Go through lists of soft skills such as those in the table above or take lists from the web and ask yourself and your colleagues the following kinds of questions:

- Do you need someone quiet or loud?
- Someone very focussed or more open to ideas?
- Someone who speaks well or is more of a good listener, or both?
- Is creativity an important quality that you need?

## Other requirements of the job

What else might your job role involve? The following are some examples of other requirements that might need to be included in a job description. The list is not exhaustive and you may think of unique factors that relate to your organization and to your particular job vacancies.

- Are the working hours unusual? Do you need somebody willing to work at weekends or overtime?
- Is there a lot of travel involved in the role and you need a candidate who is able to travel over weekends?
- Does the person need a driving licence and/or their own car?
- Do you require someone with overseas work experience?

## The complete job description

We have walked you through the key parts of a job description, namely:

- Job title and reporting line
- Tasks and responsibilities
- Skills and qualifications required
  - Education
  - Professional qualifications required
- Work experience, technical (or hard) skills required
- Soft skills and competencies required
- Other requirements of the job

Below is an example of how a completed job description can look.

---

**JOB DESCRIPTION**
**Job title:**     Business Development Manager
**Reporting to:**   Managing Director
**Tasks and responsibilities:**

- Defining the target markets and determining their market size
- Designing and implementing a customer survey to assess clients' perceptions of all aspects of our services
- Designing a group business development plan including a competitor analysis
- Being responsible for all internal communications in relation to business
- Working with all the Marketing and Sales team to secure regular referrals and to ensure appropriate follow-up

**Professional qualifications required:**

- Accountant/Lawyer/Banker background with relevant accreditation and membership(s) of associations

**Education:**

- University educated, ideally with an MBA

**Work experience:**

- At least ten years work experience
- Sound experience in sales and marketing
- Strong sense of professional integrity
- Able to conduct staff training at senior levels

**Soft skills and other requirements:**

- Speak fluent English
- Highly rational with an appreciation of practical and common-sense solutions
- Strong communication skills
- Focussed, creative and self-motivated
- Have a valid work visa

---

The job description is a very important document in any recruitment process and at a number of points in the recruitment process you will need to refer to it as you create job advertisements and interview questions.

## Avoid any discrimination issues

In most parts of the world, there are certain aspects of a candidate profile or background that employers are no longer allowed to differentiate around. These typically relate to age, marital status, race, religion, gender and sexual orientation.

As such, it is generally not accepted practice, and indeed is often illegal, to state in a job description such statements as:

- Ideal candidate will be aged under 40.
- Only single candidates should be considered.
- Female candidate preferred.

This can be illegal even if such information is not shared publically in a job advertisement, on the web or in a newspaper.

However, there are areas in which you may be able to express a preference. An example may be in terms of nationality and the desire to have only candidates who are legally able to work in your country.

## How much time do you have to fill the position?

As a rule of thumb, the more time that you can devote to the entire recruitment process, the more successful you will be in being able to find and attract an ideal candidate. This is in part because with extra time you can avoid having to rush or short-cut any parts of the recruitment process.

## How much time would you need to complete the recruitment process?

With any role, time is needed to work through the different parts of the recruitment process, which include:

- defining the job role and job description
- deciding how to source and find candidates
- finding and reviewing candidates' applications
- interviewing and selecting candidates
- reference checking the chosen candidate
- creating a job offer or letter of employment
- having the candidate accept a job offer.

In general, the recruitment process for junior or non-managerial positions can usually be completed in less than four weeks, whereas for managerial or executive level positions you might need two to three months.

## Critical job role?

Is the vacant job role a critical position – i.e. not having someone in the role is causing business difficulties, delays and leaving key work unfinished?

If this is the case, then you will want to rush and speed up the recruitment process and you may feel that 'your back is against the wall' in terms of timing. To avoid being in such a situation, you could prepare ahead of time by analysing your current organization and mapping out which roles may become vacant and, of these, which are critical roles.

The following table could be completed to help you to analyse which are the critical roles in your business and to understand where there is a high likelihood of a position becoming vacant. This is called the vacancy risk and this relates to whether you know an individual is thinking of leaving and/or there might be an upcoming discussion about whether to lay off or fire this individual.

| Vacancy risk | Role importance | | |
| --- | --- | --- | --- |
| | Low | Medium | Critical |
| High | | | |
| Medium | | | |
| Low | | | |

If you think a key job position may become vacant in the near future, you could start the recruitment process now. In such cases, the process of sourcing candidates could be started quietly and confidentially.

# What is your recruitment budget?

Before starting the process of filling a job vacancy, it is important to understand what the recruitment costs will be and how much money you are willing or able to spend. As a rule of thumb,

SUNDAY
MONDAY
TUESDAY
WEDNESDAY
THURSDAY
FRIDAY
SATURDAY

having more money at your disposal will enable you to be more successful in finding strongly qualified candidates.

What does a low cost option look like? A cheap option would be to try to fill a vacancy by finding candidates through asking around and seeking referrals from friends and colleagues. Apart from taking up your time and that of your colleagues, you may incur no other expenses, other than possibly taking out to lunch the friend who might have introduced you to the chosen final candidate.

And what does an expensive option look like? At the other extreme, you could outsource the entire process to a recruitment firm. The most expensive such firms are called executive search firms and they would typically charge your organization a fee equal to four months' salary of the chosen candidate that you hire. In addition, they may also charge you for any advertising costs.

On Monday, we help you understand how to source candidates and how to decide when you might use recruitment firms to help.

# Getting buy-in and sign-off for the recruitment process

Unless you are the boss of your company and you are the sole decision-maker, it is likely that you will need to seek the agreement and perhaps the signed approval of others. You may need to gain approval and buy-in for the:

- job description
- time frame of the recruitment
- cost of the recruitment
- other factors such as the proposed salary to be paid and the job grading to be given
- agreement of who will be involved in the recruitment process, for example who will conduct candidate interviews.

# Summary

SUNDAY

MONDAY

TUESDAY

WEDNESDAY

THURSDAY

FRIDAY

SATURDAY

This first chapter has walked you through how to start the process of recruiting to fill a particular position. This is a planning or preparation stage before jumping into the tasks of finding and interviewing potential candidates.

You can now:

● understand why you may need to hire someone to fill a job vacancy
● create a detailed and useful job description, understanding that it is made up of two key parts: a description of the job role's tasks and responsibilities; and a list of the attributes of the ideal candidate for the job

- know how to think through the timing aspects of any recruitment process, understanding how a recruitment process can take from a few days to a few months to complete
- decide if a job role is critical and determine how to plan the timing of the recruitment accordingly
- begin to appreciate the different ranges of cost that can be incurred in recruitment from a very low-cost DIY version to a more expensive version using the services of recruitment firm.

And finally it has covered the issue of agreeing with your boss and/or colleagues about the key aspects of the recruitment process.

# Questions (answers at the back)

1. Which of the following are not parts of a job description?
   a) Job title ❑
   b) Salary of the job role's direct boss ❑
   c) Job responsibilities and duties ❑
   d) Reporting line ❑

2. If your job vacancy is a critical role, how should you change your recruitment process?
   a) Only interview by telephone ❑
   b) Plan ahead of time and aim to speed up the process ❑
   c) Do not advertise the job role ❑
   d) Only have quick interviews with candidates ❑

3. Comparing the importance of the role and the risk of the role being vacant helps you determine:
   a) The length of the job description ❑
   b) How many candidates you need to source and attract ❑
   c) If the job role and potential job vacancy are critical ❑
   d) How many candidates will apply ❑

4. Which of the following are potential discrimination issues that should not be stated in a job description?
   a) Years of working experience of the candidate ❑
   b) Qualifications of the candidate ❑
   c) Marital status of the candidate ❑
   d) The type of car the candidate drives ❑

5. A person's soft skills or competencies are:
   a) The person's college qualifications ❑
   b) The person's abilities, behaviours and mind-set ❑
   c) The person's number of years of schooling ❑
   d) The person's salary level ❑

6. Before starting a recruitment process, there are two critical questions to ask. Which of the following is not such a critical question?
   a) 'Do we have a job description already prepared?' ❑
   b) 'What job role are we wishing to fill?' ❑
   c) 'The role needs to be filled by what kind of individual?' ❑
   d) 'Are you thirsty?' ❑

7. The tasks and responsibilities of a job role are:
   a) Details of what the job role involves ❑
   b) Details of the candidate's college courses ❑
   c) The components of the role's remuneration package ❑
   d) The job title of the role's boss ❑

8. The cost of a recruitment process is not determined by whether:
   a) A recruitment firm is used ❑
   b) A job is advertised in a newspaper ❑
   c) Whether your job description is old or new ❑
   d) The age of the ideal candidate ❑

# MONDAY

# How to source and find candidates

> **'Attracting top-notch talent is key in continuing to deliver superior returns for our investors.'**
>
> John Howe

This chapter explores how and where you could find candidates, by asking:

- Are there possible candidates already working in your company?
- Do you look for external candidates locally or further afield?
- Do you have a database of candidates from previous recruitments?
- Do you ask your staff to give names of people that they might know, something called employee referrals, potentially giving a financial incentive to your staff in the form of a fee for a successful referral?
- How might you contact past staff, your alumni network, to seek candidate referrals? Or perhaps contact professional associations and chambers of commerce?
- Should you be trying to find candidates at job fairs and, if you need to hire graduates, might you consider some form of campus recruitment?
- How might you work with recruitment firms to find candidates?
- Is it best to advertise your job vacancies in the newspaper and or other printed media?
- How might you use the internet and various websites to help you source candidates?
- How long will it take to find potential candidates?

# Recruit from within your organization?

Before starting to look externally or outside for candidates, I would always advise you to find out whether there are suitable candidates sitting within your own business – maybe in other departments or offices – who could be suitable for your role and for whom the new role would be a promotion (it might be hard to move someone if their current job is more senior than the one you are trying to fill).

The benefits of finding an internal candidate are:

- They already know about your organization.
- The organization already knows them.
- You do not need to invest time and money in searching externally for candidates.

Today, it is common practice to look internally as well as externally – with both internal and external candidates going through the same recruitment processes of interviewing and being assessed.

# Searching your database

I would encourage you to keep on file all candidates that have applied to your company for any reason. Such a database could be maintained online, using one of the many online candidate databases. Ideally, you could search all of the candidates by key word to find suitably qualified ones for any new job openings. Such a database could be linked to a recruitment portal or page on your company's website and each candidate applying to your company would have their CV and key information automatically saved in the database.

Note: In many countries there may be privacy and information laws relating to retaining someone's private information that you would need to abide by, for example having to give a candidate access to any information you might store about them on your database.

## Looking locally or further afield?

When planning how to find candidates from outside of your organization, an important question is from what locations are you able and willing to consider candidates?

Do you only want candidates from your town or side of the city (so that they have short commuting or travelling to work time)?

Are you more open and able to accept candidates from anywhere in your country? Or even from overseas? And in such cases, who would pay any relocation expenses?

The answer to these questions will determine how and where you will search for candidates.

# Employee referrals

You might consider asking your staff whether they know of anybody, from among their friends, ex-colleagues or family members, that they could introduce to the company as candidates for any job vacancies. Your staff understand your company's working culture and style and should be quite good judges of who can succeed in your company.

In such cases, some organizations offer a referral fee, which is paid to the employee who refers a candidate who is subsequently successfully hired. Such a payment is normally paid only after the candidate has passed a probation period (which is normally the first one to three months of employment). The fee paid might vary and might include an in-kind gift or might be paid as cash, and might equal anything up to about US$ 5,000 (around £3,000).

Do note that you will have to be diplomatic when rejecting a candidate who has been referred by an employee and you may need to personally let the employee know why their friend or family member has been rejected.

Note: I mention family members being referred but I do realize that some companies have rules on not employing close family members.

# Finding external candidates

The following sections walk you through the different methods that you can use to find external talent.

Do be ready to experiment – sometimes you will not know how successful you can be in sourcing candidates via one particular route until you have tried it. For example:

● You may not know how many candidates will respond to an advertisement until after you have actually placed the advert.
● You will not know how many suitable candidates will attend a job fair where you may wish to have a stand, until the actual day of the job fair itself.

## Recruiting from among your ex-staff

It is often quoted that your ex-staff should be ambassadors of your company. Hopefully, many of your ex-staff left on good terms and do speak positively of your company. Larger companies such as the global accounting and auditing firms maintain databases and contact with their ex-alumni and actively network with such former staff, encouraging them to return.

If you have a job vacancy, you could advertise the role to your ex-employees, via email or via an alumni website, asking them whether they are interested or if they know of others they may wish to refer. But is your company happy about re-hiring ex-staff? I ask this as some companies have a clear policy of not re-hiring their ex-employees.

## Professional associations and organizations

Are you personally, or is your company, a member of any associations and clubs through which you could advertise job vacancies? Examples of such associations might include:

● local Rotary or Lions Club
● Chambers of Commerce
● BNI Chapter or other active business referral network
● charities or foundations
● professional associations such as the Institute of Chartered Management Accountancy.

Normally such organizations would allow you, for free or for a small payment, to advertise your job vacancy. They would normally send all members the job details through a newsletter, email or posting on their website.

## State or government support

You may be able to source candidates with the help of your local authority. Examples might include:

● being able to post your job opening at a Job Centre
● subsidies or incentives available to your company if you employ a local or employ someone who is unemployed or recently released from prison.

## Job fairs

If you have a number of positions to fill, you might pay for a cubicle or stand at a relevant job or careers fair. Such fairs might be linked to a university or college (see the next section on campus recruitment) or may be arranged by a local organization. Often, such career or jobs fairs are intended to help all job-hunters to find jobs, including those who are unemployed.

## Campus recruitment

If you are seeking to employ young graduates, you might consider advertising your job vacancy with local universities or colleges. If you seek candidates with a particular degree or area of study, it might be sensible to connect with relevant departments in a university or college to seek specially qualified candidates.

## Recruitment firms

In return for a fee, a recruitment firm will help you to recruit somebody to fill your job vacancy. They can help you with all or part of the recruitment process, including tasks such as:

● creating a job description and job advertisement
● advertising the job vacancy through various channels

BLOGGS, BLOGGS & BLOGGS
SELECTION CONSULTANTS

- sourcing candidates from their own candidate databases
- carrying out initial candidate interviews
- preparing candidate written profiles
- ranking candidates
- conducting reference and background checks
- helping negotiate with the candidate that you wish to hire.

There is a growing trend for larger organizations to outsource large parts of their recruitment process to recruitment firms through a process called recruitment process outsourcing (or RPO).

Recruitment firms fall into three broad groups, which can overlap:

- Recruitment agencies
- Contingent recruitment and selection firms
- Executive search firms

Here are some details about each group:

### Recruitment agencies

Recruitment agencies help you to fill lower-level positions, normally non-managerial roles. They would typically have large databases and should be able to provide CVs of candidates within a few days of you seeking their help. Some agencies could supply you with temporary staff as well as with contract staff who may be on the payroll of the agency. (You would pay the agency a monthly fee and the agency pays the individual's salary.)

How much does it cost to use the services of a recruitment agency? As a rule of thumb, you should plan to pay the agency a fee equal to one month's salary of the individual that you successfully hire. The fee can be a little lower when you become a regular client and can be as high as two months' salary. The fee is normally only calculated on the candidate's agreed basic salary. In return, you normally agree with the agency that they will provide replacement candidates to choose from if the chosen candidate leaves within the first month of employment. This replacement period guarantee clause is very important because a proportion of newly hired staff either never turn up to work or leave after only a few days or weeks of working in your company.

To get started with a recruitment agency, you would have to sign a simple contract, agreeing to pay a fee if you hire any candidate who has been introduced to you by that agency.

You could also contract the agency to do other things such as advertising your job opening in a newspaper or on websites. You may consider such help if you have no Human Resources department and you have no time to advertise the position yourself and to deal with all the applicants that you receive.

Examples of some of the well-known global recruitment agencies include Reed, Adecco, Manpower and Kelly. In a single city, such as London, New York or Manchester, there are hundreds of agencies often specializing in certain job roles, for example there may be an agency that only helps law firms to find secretaries and personal assistants.

Finding a suitable recruitment agency is quite easy – by asking colleagues, business partners and friends, or by searching the web, Yellow Pages and classifieds jobs section in your local newspaper. In my experience, the best way of finding a suitable agency is to choose a firm that advertises a number of similar roles to that which you need to fill. Only after trying out the services of a recruitment agency will you be able to judge their level of service, quality and overall performance.

## Contingent recruitment and selection firms

Like recruitment agencies, such firms operate on what is called a contingent fee basis, which means that a fee is only payable upon the successful hiring of a candidate they have introduced to you. The fee is higher than an agency's, reflecting the focus on higher-level and harder-to-fill roles. As a rule of thumb, such firms would help you to hire professionals and mid-level managers and may, at your cost, suggest placing quite large adverts for your job vacancy in a newspaper, such as the *New York Times* or the *Guardian*, or business magazine such as the *Economist*.

Typically, such firms would find candidates through a few channels:

- advertising the position, including on their own website, on job boards
- searching their database for candidates
- searching for some candidates in the marketplace through seeking referrals as well as proactively calling potential candidates. This is the service that is provided by an executive search firm, which I describe below. Sometimes such contingent firms are called search and selection firms because of this mix of methodology that they employ.

How much does it cost to use the services of such a recruitment firm? You would typically be charged a fee that is equal to a percentage of the chosen candidate's annual salary. The percentage is typically between 15 and 25 per cent and the range of fees does vary by country, with fees being lower in this range in locations such as Australia and Singapore than in the UK, USA or Hong Kong. The recruitment firm would normally give you its standard terms and conditions, including points covering:

- the basis of the fee calculation, for example the percentage fee might be calculated on the full remuneration package including any potential bonuses
- other costs and disbursements that would be chargeable to the client
- whether, if the candidate leaves your employment within a certain time frame (normally three months), they will find a free replacement candidate for you.

Be ready to negotiate the level of fee. You may try to agree a fee that is a fixed amount of money and/or is a percentage based only on the base salary.

Examples of such firms include Robert Half, Harvey Nash and Hays. Although not as numerous as recruitment agencies, many exist in each major city or even town and may not be distinguishable from recruitment agencies in terms of their brand offerings.

However, I would recommend only choosing and working with one contingent recruitment and selection firm on an exclusive basis to avoid a situation of candidates being approached by more than one recruitment firm.

## Executive search firms (also called headhunting firms)

You would typically consider using such a firm if your vacant job position were senior and potentially hard to fill, and as a rule of thumb you might use such a firm for senior managerial, director or C-level (CEO, COO and so on) positions. You may also choose to use such a firm for very specialized and hard-to-fill non-managerial positions such a specialist or niche positions where there may be very few candidates.

Such firms may also be referred to as retained executive search or retained search firms. The term 'retained' refers to the fact that a client will have to retain their services by paying the total fee, which is normally equal to one third of the chosen candidate's total annual remuneration (the fee is typically between 30 and 35 per cent).

The search firm would offer you the following:

● Proactively find suitable candidates for the role through a combination of using their database and making cold calls to potential candidates (in relevant roles and organizations). You would pre-agree with the search firm's consultant where they would look for candidates, for example possibly searching in your competitors' businesses.
● Find a free replacement candidate if the chosen placed candidate leaves your company, typically within the first six months. This guarantee period is long because with senior staff it takes some time to work out whether they are a good fit and are able to perform well.

Examples of the globally located executive search firms include Korn/Ferry, Egon Zehnder, Spencer Stuart and Russell Reynolds. Far fewer such firms exist, compared to the contingent recruitment firms.

With all kinds of recruitment firms you would normally work with a recruitment consultant or headhunter. They may hold manager, director or partner titles and they should personally do the following:

● talk with you to understand your company and the job vacancy
● negotiate the terms and conditions with respect to their company's services
● work with their colleagues to write job advertisements, source candidates through advertising and searching their own company's database
● interview all the candidates that they present to you and write summary profiles about each candidate, which explain why the candidate is a good fit
● directly communicate with the candidates up to the moment they have begun working with your company and during their probation period.

# Advertising your position

You may have the time and resources to advertise the job vacancy directly in a newspaper, journal or on certain websites. Look to see how similar positions are being advertised in your location and/or industry before committing to an advertising agreement or contract. The key questions to consider are:

● What print media and which websites would potential candidates visit? Where would they go to look for a job?
● What is the cost of advertising compared to the number of potential candidates who might see the advert? (You could calculate a cost per applicant.)

Creating a job advertisement for posting on a website or for putting in the print media is quite easy if you have already created a job description. The next chapter will share how

to ensure that any job advertisement that you create is as effective and impactful as possible in impressing and attracting the ideal candidates.

# Finding candidates on the internet

There are three main groups of websites that can help you with your recruitment:

- jobsites (also called job boards)
- social networking sites such as LinkedIn.com
- your own company website and blog.

In the next chapter, when we look at your branding, we cover the latter two groups of websites; here we now explore how you can use a jobsite.

## Using jobsites

Also referred to as job boards or job-listing websites, there are hundreds of such jobsites existing all over the world with many listing thousands of job openings posted by employers or by recruitment firms.

    You can use such websites in two ways:

## 1 Search the website candidate database for suitable candidates.

Rather like carrying out a detailed internet search, you would typically enter keywords such as job title, location, industry and so on to find potentially suitable candidates. This process can be very time consuming, particularly if your search results give you hundreds of possible candidates.

A common headache is having to communicate with many of these candidates, asking them by email (or via the website) whether they are interested in the job vacancy that you have open. You will probably find that most of these passive candidates have no interest and may not even reply to you.

## 2 Post a job advertisement.

Rather than searching for candidates yourself, let the interested candidates come to you. You place a job advertisement on the jobsite and can have the candidates send applications to your email (or they can sit in your account on that particular jobsite, for you to review in your own time).

### Types of jobsites

Every week, new jobsites appear online and others disappear. Here is a list of some of the well-established and popular sites:

| Jobsites covering all sectors and industries and covering many countries | Jobs.com<br>Careerbuilder.com<br>Monster.com<br>Jobsdb.com<br>Totaljobs.com<br>Seek.com.au<br>Jobcircle.com |
|---|---|
| Industry specific jobsites | Engineeringjobs.co.uk<br>Salesvacancies.com |
| City or region specific sites | Cityjobs.com<br>Londonjobs.co.uk<br>Newyorkrecruiter.com |
| Newspapers' online job boards | Jobs.guardian.co.uk<br>Jobmarket.nytimes.com |

How much can you expect to pay to post a job on such job board websites? Normally, the cost of posting a single job is less than US$100–200 (£50–150). The cost of searching the database of candidates can vary and is sometimes free if you are paying for a job posting but you may be limited to only being able to connect with a certain number of candidates on the database.

## How much time is needed to find candidates?

As a rule of thumb, the more senior the position the longer it will take to find candidates and it is normally quicker if you use a recruitment firm to help you advertise and to find candidates for you:

- Finding candidates for a junior administration clerk, receptionist, secretary or driver position may only take a couple of days.
- Sourcing candidates for a sales manager position might take a few weeks or months.
- Finding suitable candidates to fill a senior vice president or managing director position might take three to six months with the help of an executive search firm.

# Summary

Be ready to adopt a multi-pronged strategy and consider using a few recruitment channels simultaneously. We have explored how and where you could find and attract candidates for your job openings:

- We discussed how you should check whether there are suitable candidates within your company and within your database of candidates.

- In terms of looking for external candidates, we shared how you must decide where candidates can come in a geographic sense, whether you only want candidates who are located nearby or whether you are happy with candidates coming from further afield.

- We have shown how employee referrals can be a good and cost-effective source of candidates.

- Your ex-staff can also be valuable sources of contacts and referrals and you may even consider employing an ex-staff.

SUNDAY
MONDAY
TUESDAY
WEDNESDAY
THURSDAY
FRIDAY
SATURDAY

- We have demonstrated the many other possible sources of candidates that you could use, including professional associations and Chambers of Commerce, as well as attending job fairs.

- For those of you needing to hire graduates, we discussed about how you might connect with universities and colleges.

- You will now understand the different types of recruitment firms, from agencies through to executive search firms, and how you might consider working with them.

- We explored how you might advertise in various print media, including newspapers.

- Last but not least, we covered the growing area of the internet and showed you the many ways in which you can advertise jobs and find candidates on various kinds of websites, from job boards through to using your own company website.

# Questions (answers at the back)

1. Which recruitment firms charge the lowest fee?
   a) Recruitment agencies ❏
   b) Contingent selection firms ❏
   c) Executive search firms ❏
   d) All the firms charge the same fees ❏

2. The replacement guarantee period offered by a recruitment agency is normally:
   a) One day ❏
   b) One month ❏
   c) One year ❏
   d) One week ❏

3. Jobsites are useful to:
   a) Advertise job vacancies ❏
   b) Interview candidates ❏
   c) Conduct reference checks ❏
   d) Carry out reference checks ❏

4. An executive search firm will not:
   a) Advertise your job vacancy ❏
   b) Proactively search for candidates ❏
   c) Help you to lay off the person occupying the job role ❏
   d) Charge a retainer fee ❏

5. What is a benefit of searching for candidates among your current or ex-staff?
   a) They are cheaper ❏
   b) They should know your company well ❏
   c) They have better educational qualifications ❏
   d) They will stay with your company longer ❏

6. One way of searching for candidates that was recommended in this chapter is to:
   a) Ask your competitor to give you their employees' names ❏
   b) Advertise through professional associations ❏
   c) Contact candidates that you had fired for poor performance ❏
   d) Go into the street and shout out that you seek candidates ❏

7. Which type of recruitment firm would normally offer the longest replacement period guarantee for a newly hired candidate?
   a) Executive search firm ❏
   b) Recruitment agency ❏
   c) Contingent selection firm ❏
   d) None of the above ❏

8. With candidates who apply to your company, you are recommended to:
   a) Throw away their applications ❏
   b) Keep them on a database ❏
   c) Ignore them ❏
   d) Interview all of them ❏

9. Normally, which of the following job vacancies would take the longest to fill?
   a) Secretary ❏
   b) Accountant ❏
   c) Managing Director ❏
   d) Receptionist ❏

# TUESDAY

**How to attract candidates and to create a strong employer brand**

> *'The key for us, number one, has always been hiring very smart people.'*
> Bill Gates

> *'Time spent on hiring is time well spent.'*
> Robert Half

Attracting an individual to work for your company is quite similar to trying to entice someone to buy your products or services. In spite of unemployment levels, in most countries, being viewed as too high, there is, to quote the global consulting firm Mckinsey, an ongoing war for talent. Talented individuals have choices and you must work on the assumption that attracting an ideal candidate will involve effort, just as it does to attract and win a good new client.

In this chapter, we will help you to understand how to optimize what is called your employer branding. This will involve:

- Understanding and learning from why you and your colleagues chose to work at your organization
- Creating a 20-seconds sales pitch
- Ensuring you have impactful job advertisements
- Making sure that your corporate or company website is attractive and inviting to jobseekers and to those you are wanting to join your company
- Maximizing your company's presence on the internet, including on social networking sites

We then explore how to attract the largest group of potential applicants for any job openings that you may have – the internet-savvy Generation Y.

# Optimizing your employer brand

All sales and marketing involves attracting customers and encouraging them to buy your products. Organizations create and maintain what is called a brand or branding strategy, where a brand is made up of a combination of what a potential or actual customer:

● thinks and understands
● perceives and observes
● is promised and expects.

If you have never tried a product before, how did you decide to buy it? Was it from:

● seeing some advertising and marketing materials?
● referrals and comments from other users?
● seeing other people using the product and service?

Let us now imagine that the product or service being offered is a job at a company. The company needs to market the job opportunity to you, in the hope that you will 'buy' the opportunity, that is, apply for the role and later accept a job offer.

A company's employer branding is the combination of ways in which a company is able to both attract potential employees and is able to retain them, as satisfied 'customers'. The employer branding is sometimes referred to as the complete package of benefits offered to a potential employee.

Note: In this chapter, we are focussing on the employer brand in terms of how you attract people to work in your organization. Later, on Saturday, we will explore your employer branding in terms of how do you retain your newly hired staff – asking are your new staff actually experiencing and being offered what they expected when they were being recruited by you?

How is the employer branding useful? An optimal employer branding can help ensure that you both:

● attract enough candidate applications
● have strongly qualified candidates accept your job offers.

## What is your employer branding?

An easy way to explore this question is to ask yourself: *'Why do people choose to work at our company (or organization)?'*

Think back to when you were looking for a new job and you chose to work at your current employer. Were you fresh out of university or school? Or had you been working for many years in a few different organizations?

Make a list of the reasons why you chose to work for your current employer. These might include:

● You liked the company's logo and website content.
● The office was walking distance from your home.
● You liked the company's canteen.
● The person who would be your boss seemed really nice.
● You would be given travel opportunities.
● They offered a good pension scheme.
● You loved their products.
● They had nice work stations.
● They offered you a great starting salary.

Ask some of your colleagues, of all ages, why they chose to work for your company. Are they giving similar answers to you?

SUNDAY
MONDAY
TUESDAY
WEDNESDAY
THURSDAY
FRIDAY
SATURDAY

Are you able to see any reasons that attracted a number of people? Perhaps:

- The office layout and large work stations attracted people.
- Good medical benefits were a common reason for people accepting job offers.
- Many liked the personalities of the interviewers.
- The exciting product range attracted many.

Take a look at the organizations that are trying to hire similar staff to yours. They may be competitors or may be in other fields. How do they seem to attract people to join them? Do their websites reveal anything? Take a look at their job advertisements on the internet or in newspapers – how do such companies describe themselves? What do they offer that you could copy or improve upon?

Write down your employer branding, making notes of how certain parts might be maintained, strengthened and improved. You could use a template like this:

| Employer branding component | Notes |
| --- | --- |
|  |  |
|  |  |
|  |  |

I would strongly advise you to improve your employer branding in two ways:

- **Maximize the content:** What more can you offer to potential staff? It is important to aim for a situation where your job vacancies and your company are viewed by job-hunters at least as favourably as other companies' job openings that they might be applying for.
- **Optimize how you present the content:** How can you improve the ways in which you present your offerings in the most impactful and optimal ways? There are two key areas in which you present yourselves, and we explore these below:
  - in your job advertisements
  - in your general marketing materials, including the contents of your corporate websites and brochures.

# Your 20-seconds elevator sales pitch

When job-seekers are looking for job openings, they will probably be overwhelmed by the number of jobs that they could choose to apply for. You have to assume that they will not spend a long time looking at your job advertisements, your company websites or in reading any internet search results for your company and so on.

Imagine a street full of shops all selling the same products and you own one of those shops. How do you invite someone to step into your shop when they will only spend a few seconds passing your shop window?

I recommend that you create a short summary of the key parts of your employer branding in what I call your 20-seconds elevator sales pitch. In the above 'shopping' example, your sales pitch is what you would place in your window display in order to entice passers-by to enter your shop. It is similar to the idea of summarizing your unique selling propositions (or USPs).

Note: The original idea of an elevator sales pitch came from how you could market and sell an idea to somebody while you both shared a short elevator ride lasting just 20 seconds.

What is your 20-seconds elevator sales pitch?

Part should relate to your company and part should relate to the actual job opening. Here are some examples of wording that could form part of such a sales pitch:

- We are a well-established leader in our field of ...
- We have a fun and caring open-plan work culture where we quickly reward great work and great ideas.
- We have a modern office near the train station, with a canteen full of fresh food.
- We have a flat management structure where your voice will be heard.

You will note that the above statements are company-focussed and the following are job-role specific, in this example for the role of a Business Development Manager (for the job description shared in Sunday's chapter):

- We will support and pay for your professional development through an Executive MBA or other professional course.
- You will be given overseas travel opportunities.
- You will have sole responsibility for creating a new sales management model.
- You will work closely with the Board of Directors in helping to grow the business into new overseas markets.

Try writing down a 20-seconds elevator sales pitch for a job opening you have. It could be written as a short paragraph or as five to ten bullet-point sentences.

We will now explore the many ways in which you use your sales pitch wording:

- in job advertisements (see below)
- on your company website and other websites (see below)
- during your interviewing process (see Wednesday).

# Creating job advertisements with impact

Unless you can attract candidates through word of mouth referrals, you will need some of written job advertisement.

How can you create a complete and clear job advert for any job opening? The following table summarizes what I would suggest you include:

| The job advertisement's content | Source of information |
|---|---|
| Job title (and reporting line) | Maybe your company has rules on job titles that can be used |
| 1–2 short paragraphs and/or a few bullet points detailing: *your company, including why it is a great company to work for* *why the job opening is exciting and interesting* | From your 20-seconds elevator sales pitch (which comes from your employer branding) |
| Tasks and responsibilities of the job role – normally as bullet points | From the job description (which we described on Sunday) |
| The skills and qualifications required – normally as bullet points | From the job description |
| Other content might include: *salary and remuneration details* *how to apply, including deadline* *request for references* | |

## Example of a job advertisement

This example links to the example of the Business Development Manager job description from Sunday's chapter.

**Business Development Manager**

Reporting to the Managing Director

We are a well-established leader in our field of Accounting Software, where your career can truly excel.

Do you want to work in a fun and caring open-plan work culture where great work and great ideas are always rewarded?

In a flat management structure where your voice would always be heard?

Do you want to work in an office that provides a great canteen and within easy walking distance of the station?

If you become our Business Development Manager, we can offer you some outstanding career opportunities, including: supporting and paying for your professional development through an Executive MBA or other professional courses; providing many overseas travel opportunities; giving you the opportunity to create a new sales management model and enabling you to work closely with the Board of Directors in helping to grow the business into new overseas markets.

Other key tasks and responsibilities of the role will include:

- defining the target markets and determining their market size
- designing and implementing a customer survey to assess clients' perceptions of all aspects of our services
- designing a group business development plan including a competitor analysis.

**To be considered for this exciting role, we seek an experienced sales and marketing executive from either the legal, accounting or banking sectors.**

If you are a strong candidate, you will probably have a degree with at least ten years of work experience, a strong sense of professional integrity and be able to conduct staff training at senior levels. Speaking fluent English, you will be good at creating practical and common-sense solutions and you will be focussed, creative and self-motivated.

A competitive remuneration package is offered.

Please apply to Mrs Angela Smith, HR Manager at asmith@xxxxxx.com, sending a copy of your CV. We will reply to all applications received before the deadline of 15 October.

## Additional tips

From the above example, you might notice:

- To show that the role is senior, I mention in the second line to whom the role reports. If your job opening is not senior, you may choose not to mention to whom it reports.
- The first two paragraphs are taken from the 20-seconds elevator sales pitch.
- I try to make the opening paragraph of the advert stand out by asking questions. You or a colleague with a marketing background may be able to produce wording with even more impact.
- I try to make the wording easy to read and interesting.

SUNDAY

MONDAY

TUESDAY

WEDNESDAY

THURSDAY

FRIDAY

SATURDAY

Try writing a job advertisement for your job opening and ask your colleagues for their input. The above example is simply that – an example! Each job advertisement is unique and yours will reflect the uniqueness of your job opening and of your company's culture, working style and so on.

You can use your job advertisement to advertise the job opening in any of the places that we explored in the previous chapter. You could also pass the advert wording to a recruitment firm that you may choose to work with, asking them to use the advert wording. Such a firm, from their experience, may be able to make the wording more attractive and impactful.

## Optimizing your company website and web presence

Potential applicants to your company will probably visit your company's website and/or may carry out an internet search of your company.

Does your company's website present the right messages and image? It may primarily exist to help promote your products and services, but it is also promoting or reflecting your employer branding (and sales pitch). After visiting your site, will a potential job applicant feel more positive about applying to your company or not?

Even if you are small company with a limited budget for your website, there are a few things that I would encourage you to include on your corporate website:

- Firstly, do have a corporate website!
- Include a section of 'Why work here?' and have quotes and videos of staff sharing why they like to work in the company.
- Try to include aspects of your employer branding in the website, for example if you claim that your company is a fun place to work in, then ensure that your website appears fun.
- If you include an online job application process, do make it easy and ensure that anybody who has applied through your website receives an email confirmation from a real person and not just automated emails.

If you are not sure of what excellent corporate websites look like, visit the sites of any of the world's leading companies such as Virgin, General Electric, Microsoft and British Airways. Also explore why some companies win awards with titles such as 'Employer of the Year'.

Also type into an internet search engine phrases such as 'why work at ...' or 'employer of choice' to see what kinds of words and images are used by other companies that you could copy or even improve upon.

Likewise in your area of business and location, what are your competitors' websites looking like?

Explore other ways in which you might make use of the internet to attract more applicants, with possible ideas including:

- advertising jobs through LinkedIn and creating a company page on this free business networking site. There are many other similar sites such as bing.com

- creating a company page on Facebook or any of the other social networking sites
- recruiting and conducting interviews on websites such as secondlife.com, where one has an avatar to represent you.

# How to brand your company and attract Generation Y

We cannot give you a complete guidebook to recruitment, without exploring how you can optimally recruit the Gen-Y or New Millenials or what are also called the Net Generation. This typically refers to those born after 1980 and are those workers who are today in their twenties.

As an average rule of thumb, 80 per cent of job vacancies today are filled with candidates aged in their twenties, given that we typically hire younger staff to fill trainee non-managerial positions and we try to retain these staff to eventually take on more senior positions.

This entire book will help you to hire the Gen-Y as well as older generations, but here are some tips about how to attract the Gen-Y in particular.

They live on the internet and are very internet and computer knowledgeable – they are far more likely to read about your company on the web than they are in the newspaper or even in your company brochures. As a result, it is even more important to ensure that your company's web presence is as optimal as possible.

Studies are showing that the Gen-Y have different expectations to older generations. You may need to offer what the Gen-Y want and to ensure that your employer branding and any sales pitch reflects this. From my experience, the younger job-hunters seek the following when looking for a job:

- early and quick responsibility
- supportive bosses and 'pats on the back'
- nice working environment
- variety of tasks and activities.

On the downside, it seems that the Gen-Y may not have the loyalty or staying power to remain with one employer for very long.

How might you tailor your advertising and branding to ensure that you appeal to this Gen-Y cohort?

# Summary

There is an ongoing war for talent and good candidates always seem to be in short supply. This chapter has hopefully given you some good ideas and tips on how you can maximize any candidate attraction and advertising campaigns.

After working through this chapter, you should now be able to:

● understand what employer branding is and be able to explore how you can maximize your company's employer branding
● write an effective 20-seconds elevator sales pitch, which in just a few lines can explain why a person should consider working for your company and also why they should apply for a particular job vacancy
● produce an impactful and well-written job advertisement, which uses the content of the sales pitch and of the job description
● ensure that your company's website and web presence can be maximized so that the messaging is appealing to any potential candidates and is in line with your desired employer branding messaging
● understand how you might need to tailor your recruitment for the Generation Y job-hunters.

SUNDAY
MONDAY
TUESDAY
WEDNESDAY
THURSDAY
FRIDAY
SATURDAY

# Questions (answers at the back)

1. An employer brand is useful to:
a) Attract candidates to apply to work for your company ❏
b) Help determine what remuneration should be paid ❏
c) Decide when to fill a job vacancy ❏
d) Determine the salary level ❏

2. Your job vacancy focussed 20-seconds elevator sales pitch is based upon:
a) Your competitors' employer branding ❏
b) Your own organization's employer branding ❏
c) How you recruit to fill the role ❏
d) The time of year ❏

3. The Generation Y, or Gen-Y, differ from older employees in terms of:
a) Having different expectations ❏
b) Not being comfortable using the internet ❏
c) Not liking job interviews ❏
d) Working slower ❏

4. The job advertisement is not based upon which of the following:
a) Job description ❏
b) Employer branding and the sales pitch ❏
c) Letter of termination ❏
d) Salary slip ❏

5. What approximate proportion of job roles are filled with Gen-Y candidates, aged in their twenties?
a) 50 per cent ❏
b) 80 per cent ❏
c) 100 per cent ❏
d) None ❏

6. Your company or corporate website should include a section that answers the question:
a) Who are your competitors? ❏
b) Why does your company pay low salaries? ❏
c) Why work here? ❏
d) Why do staff leave the company? ❏

7. A job advertisement can be posted on all the following except:
a) Your competitor's corporate website ❏
b) Jobsites or job boards ❏
c) Your own recruiting section of your company website ❏
d) In the local newspaper ❏

8. An effective employer branding:
a) Attracts staff to consider leaving your company ❏
b) Attracts candidates to apply to work for your company ❏
c) Will make it slower to hire new staff ❏
d) Attacts no one ❏

9. Should a job advertisement include the role's job title?
a) Yes ❏
b) No ❏
c) Sometimes ❏
d) Not sure ❏

# WEDNESDAY

# How to interview with success

> *'Hiring people is an art, not a science, and resumes [CVs] can't tell you whether someone will fit into a company's culture.'*
>
> Howard Schultz

Interviews are the most important part of the recruitment process – it is the only time when you can actually have a long conversation with a candidate to truly explore whether you think that they are able and willing to do the job and if they will fit well into your company. Unlike when reading a CV or an email from a candidate, during an interview you can get a better sense of the person's personality and character.

This chapter will explore:

- How you decide who you actually interview and what to tell those who are not chosen for interview
- Learning how to read a candidate's CV and reading between the lines of what the candidate has stated or has not stated
- The interview preparation process, including deciding who will conduct any interviews and in what form
- Sharing the different types of interviewing models and questions and deciding what each candidate will be asked
- Understanding that all impressions count and that the interview is a two-way process with you, the employer, needing to impress the candidates, as much as they need to impress you

# Selecting candidates for interview

## If you are working with a recruitment firm

If you use a recruitment firm to help you with your recruitment process, you could ask the recruitment firm to receive and vet all applications and to select the most suitable applicants for you to interview. The recruitment firm will have the challenge of searching through and filtering all the applicants that they can find. In such cases, it is very important that your contact point at the recruitment firm truly understands what the profile is for the ideal candidate.

## If you are not using a recruitment firm

Assuming that you are not using the services of a recruitment firm, you will have more work to do. You or one of your colleagues will have to receive and sort out the emails or letters of applications in response to job advertisements that you have placed on the web or in printed media.

I would strongly recommend that you request that applicants only apply via email or via a website portal (on your own company's website or on a job board website such as monster.com). I believe that the days of sending written applications by post are almost over but there are some employers who still encourage applications in hard copy.

How many applicants can you expect to receive? It is difficult to give a precise answer but I would suggest that for a position advertised on a well-known jobs board website you will receive between 50 and over 200 applications for a single job posting.

## How do you select candidates for interview?

It is highly unlikely that you will wish to interview all applicants! As a rule of thumb, you and/or colleagues may wish to meet face to face with up to ten of the most strongly qualified candidates.

An objective way of selecting candidates for interview is to use a score sheet to rank all the candidates. Let me explain this by giving an example using the job advertisement that we looked at in the previous chapter, which you will recall was based on the job description from Sunday. Taking all the candidate requirements listed in the job advert, I could produce a ranking of all the ideal candidate's requirements in order of importance such as:

Applicant Ranking Criteria Sheet

For candidate_____

| Order of importance | Criteria | Score (Circle number if candidate fulfils criteria) |
| --- | --- | --- |
| 1 | Worked in legal/banking/accounting sectors | 5 |
| 2 | Sales and marketing background | 4 |
| 3 | At least ten years of working experience | 3 |
| 4 | Speaks native/fluent English | 2 |
| 5 | Has sales training experience | 1 |
| | TOTAL SCORE | |

You could choose any number of criteria and you could change the scoring as you wish – for example, you might decide that 'worked in the legal/banking/accounting sectors' is extremely essential and you could change the score of 5 to a 10.

You might also decide to conduct quick telephone interviews with those candidates who are borderline and who you are not sure whether you should interview. Such telephone interviews allow you to clarify points that may not be clear in their CV.

Such an objective approach to selection can be time–consuming as you have to skim-read many CVs, but has a number of benefits:

● You avoid overlooking a suitable candidate because such a process forces you to look at each CV in a systematic way.
● You avoid any future claims of discrimination by being able to prove you were being objective and systematic.
● You can then follow this up by being equally systematic with those candidates that you choose to interview (which we explore later in this chapter).

# Communicating with all applicants

It is very important to send polite responses, by email, to all applicants who are not being selected for interview. From my experience, so many applicants for job vacancies send in their applications and never hear anything from either the employer or from a recruitment firm. At best, they may only receive an automated 'thank you for your CV' email.

If you are using a recruitment firm, you should request that the team in the firm reply politely to all applicants even if they are not being selected to meet with you and your colleagues. For those candidates that you have selected for an interview, you could inform them of this decision by email, but I would strongly recommend that you or one of your colleagues call them to invite them for interview and then to follow this up with an email. This is more polite and warmer but, on a more practical level, you can also use the phone calls to check the candidates' communication skills and telephone skills. You may find that a candidate who states 'Has fluent English' on their CV, may not be so fluent after all. This leads to the next section on understanding candidates' CVs.

# Reading and understanding CVs

I have had the pleasure of reading thousands of CVs of all shapes and sizes – some might be over 20 pages long.

I have learned the following tips about how to ensure that you can read a CV well and how to spot any anomalies:

- Strong candidates for a job opening may not know how to write an impressive CV. Some experienced professionals and managers believe that a good CV should be at least 10 pages long and list every detail of each job they have held. I would look for great content and not great presentation when deciding which candidates to interview. However, you can ask a candidate in an interview about their CV to help understand why they may have created a poor-quality CV. There is a common understanding that a good CV should be two to three pages long, but this is not something that everyone is taught.
- Candidates may over-exaggerate their job title and/or job responsibilities. Some job-seekers can be desperate for a new job and may resort to lying about their work experience. Sometimes an interviewer will miss this and it may even be missed in reference checking (covered in the next chapter).

Be aware of errors and omissions on a CV. A common example is for candidates to hide periods of unemployment on their CV and lie about the dates when they were employed in different roles. Assuming that they are honest about the dates when they were employed, you can spot periods between jobs that you can ask the candidate about in the interview.

Avoid discriminating based upon the personal details shown on a CV. Avoid the common tendency of accepting or rejecting candidates for interview based on whether they are married, whether they are male or female, based on their looks (from a photo on their CV) or based on their religion and so on. I strongly encourage you to filter all applicants' CVs based only on the ranking of the key job requirements criteria that I have discussed above.

# Preparing for an interview

In my experience, I realize that managers and executives are always very busy and generally find it hard to make time to interview candidates well. A large part of the problem is a lack of good preparation before the interviews actually take place.

## How do you prepare well for a series of interviews?

● **Communicating with candidates:** When inviting candidates for interview, what information needs to be shared with them? Do they need to be asked to bring any copies of references, educational certificates and so on?

- **Interview location:** Do decide where interviews will be held and if necessary book the chosen meeting room. Many times I have seen candidates come to companies for interviews only to discover there is no meeting room booked. Try to ensure that the room will be clean and tidy in order to give candidates a positive impression.

- **Length of interview:** How long do you wish the first initial interviews to last? Between 45–60 minutes is a typical length of an initial interview. It is good practice to warn the candidates how long the interview is expected to last.

- **Choice of interviewers and style of interview:** How many people will interview the candidate in the first round? Might it just be the HR Manager and/or the manager to whom the successful candidate would later report? Will you have a group or panel interview with more than one interviewer?

- **Number of times a candidate will be interviewed:** Will it be acceptable if candidates are only interviewed once before an offer is made? This might be fine for more junior level positions such as for the role of driver or receptionist. However, I would strongly recommend that you conduct second or even third interviews for most positions, if only to give the candidate time to get to know your company (I explain why in the next chapter).

- **Type of interview:** If a face-to-face interview is not possible, perhaps due to the candidate or interviewer being out of town or in a different location, will there be an interview over the phone or via video conferencing (e.g. using Skype)? Such remote interviews may not give you as good an understanding of the candidate compared to a face-to-face interview in which you can observe all the body language of the candidate.

- **Preparing the interviewers:** Who will make sure that each interviewer is given copies of the candidates' CVs plus copies of the job description? In the next section, we explain the important topic of how the interviewers will conduct the interview, including what questions can be asked and what notes should be taken.

# Types of interview questions

There is no best practice rule about what kinds of questions you should ask candidates, but it is very useful to understand the following kinds of questioning that can be used.

Any question is either closed-ended or open-ended:

- Closed-ended questions – these are simple questions that only require a 'Yes' or 'No' type of answer. They are useful for clarifying simple facts such as:
  - Are you a qualified accountant?
  - Do you have your own car?
  - Are you happy to travel with your work?
- Open-ended questions – such questions compel the candidate to answer with more than a simple 'Yes' or 'No'. Examples might start with:
  - Tell me more about...
  - What is your opinion of...
  - How did you overcome...

As a rule of thumb an open-ended question can teach you more about a candidate than simply asking a 'Yes' or 'No' type of question.

Effective interviewing questions are normally a mix of what are called behavioural, situational and outcome-based questions. In simple terms, such questions are intended to better understand the candidate's work experiences in order to help answer the key question of *'Could the candidate do well in our company and when employed in the job (vacancy)?'*

Behavioural questions focus on a candidate's behaviours and competencies. They help seek evidence that the candidate has, and is able to use, particular behaviours or competencies. Examples of such questions might include:

- How persistent are you?
- Give me examples of when you have been very persistent?
- Have you ever led a team?
- How did you communicate with and motivate the team?

Situational questions explore how the candidate coped with a certain situation. You might ask questions such as:

- Tell me about a time when you were leading a project. How did you respond to all the issues and challenges?
- How did you cope with stressful situations? Please give examples.

Outcome-based questions are for learning about what were the outcomes achieved by the candidate in various work situations. Such questions might include:

- What did you learn from leading the team during the budgeting process?
- What were the results of your sales efforts last year with your technical sales team?

## Planning your interview questions

I recommend that you decide what information you need to help you to choose the most suitable candidate(s) to fill your job vacancy. You then need to decide what form of questions you need to ask the candidates to try to gather this necessary information.

I strongly encourage you to be as systematic as possible and to follow this two-step model:

- Step 1: List information needed – in terms of the candidates' experiences, background, skills and competencies that are required to perform the job well. This comes from the job description that you will already have drawn up.
- Step 2: List questions to ask in the interview – involves developing the questions that you will have to ask in order to be able to seek the evidence and information that the candidate has the right experiences, background and skills and so on.

Working with the Business Development Manager job position that we have been using to date in this book, here is a summary of how you could use this two-step model.

| Step 1 Information needed | Step 2 Questions to ask |
|---|---|
| Sound experience in sales and marketing | Could you tell me about your key successes in your sales role? How you have managed to win some new key accounts? What kinds of marketing initiatives have you implemented? |
| Able to conduct staff trainings | In what ways are you a good trainer? Give examples of sales trainings that you have conducted. What kinds of results have you achieved with such trainings? How did you measure the improvement in the performance of staff that you trained? |
| Strong communication skills | Share how you would talk with one of your team who is not performing well. How do you communicate with clients who may be complaining or upset with your company's services? |
| Strong sense of personal integrity | How would you respond if a buying manager at a client was to ask you to thank them in some way for passing your company some new business? |

## Additional areas of questioning

In addition to asking the above questions, which are seeking evidence that the candidate can fulfil the job requirements, there are a few other areas of questioning that you may need to cover in the interviews to help answer the following kinds of concerns:

- Why is the candidate job hunting?
- Can the candidate fit into our team and working culture?
- Will the candidate be accepted and liked?
- Is the candidate really interested in our job vacancy and company?
- Have they bothered to do any research about our company?

- When could the candidate start work with us?
- Does the candidate have any questions they would like to ask?

You could ask these in the first interview or in later interviews.

## Interview notes

I would urge you to create and have typed up a list of interview questions for a particular role, and that you ask each candidate the same questions and keep notes on their answers. This will allow you to objectively compare each candidate in order to choose which ones you might shortlist for further interviews and which candidates you will reject.

You should also record notes about each candidate's overall presentation style and personality with possible comments such as:

- seems very positive
- very nervous
- seems very interested in role and did a lot of research
- does not listen well
- speaks too much
- has a weak handshake

Be careful not to list comments that could be viewed as discriminatory, for example 'he acted very feminine', or 'she has too many children'.

# Understanding the two-way nature of Interviews

Candidates will come to your job interviews with the intention of impressing you and your colleagues. One would hope that the candidate would come well attired and groomed and well prepared.

You must also aim to come to the interview with the aim of impressing the candidate and of ensuring that the candidate has a very positive impression of your company. This connects to trying to have a good employer branding.

Here are some pointers about how you and your colleagues can create an optimal impression.

Interviewers should prepare well for the interview:

● Read the candidate's CV and any application (e.g. email).
● Read the job description.
● Prepare, understand and use specific interview questions.

At the interview, the interviewers should:

- dress professionally
- be on time and polite
- try to make the candidate feel at ease and start the interview by simply chatting rather than jumping into any difficult questions
- show genuine interest in the candidate.

In addition:

- ensure that the candidate is met and treated well before the interview
- offer the candidate a drink and the chance to freshen up in the toilet
- decide whether the candidate will be shown around the company or office as part of the interview process
- remember the saying that all impressions count!

# Additional interviews

It is normal for a company to interview some candidates more than once before being able to choose which candidate to make an offer to.

There are no fixed rules, but as an example you may meet eight candidates in a first round of interviewing. You may then meet the strongest three candidates for second interviews before inviting one back for a final, third interview.

Some organizations, such as investment banks, may have a rule that each candidate should meet at least five people in separate interviews before they can be hired. In smaller organizations, one interview might be all that is required.

I would recommend having at least two interviews, with the stronger or more preferred candidates, in order to enable:

- other colleagues to also meet the candidates
- the candidates to get to know you all a little better – by the second interview they may also have thought of some important questions
- you to get to know the candidates better.

# Summary

This chapter has walked you through the entire interviewing process and you will now realize that interviewing is not simply about 'turning up' to an interview, but is also about good preparation and being systematic.

You are now able to interview candidates very effectively and professionally, including:

● being able to select certain candidates for interview using an objective ranking system that can remove any subjective bias

● understanding the importance of and knowing how to communicate with all applicants, including those that are not being interviewed and are being rejected

● being alert to how a candidate's CV might include discrepancies and mistakes that you can bring up at interview

● realizing why and how to be very well prepared for the interviewing process, including reading all relevant materials and preparing specific interview questions that are directly linked to the requirements of your job vacancy

SUNDAY
MONDAY
TUESDAY
WEDNESDAY
THURSDAY
FRIDAY
SATURDAY

- asking additional interview questions in order to explore whether the candidate is both interested in your job role and company and whether they will fit well into your company

- creating a positive impression for the candidate with an understanding that you need to impress, as much as the candidate needs to impress you

- recording notes from each of your interviews as an objective record to be used when selecting which candidates will be rejected and which will be asked for further interviews and so on.

# Questions (answers at the back)

1. When selecting candidates for interview, it is recommended that a systematic method is used to:
a) Show which candidates are lying on their CVs ❑
b) Rank candidates according to how well they fit with the job requirements ❑
c) Find out which candidate is interested in your company ❑
d) Rank candidates by their age ❑

2. Interview notes are useful:
a) To give email feedback to candidates ❑
b) To show the candidates after the interview ❑
c) To be able to select which candidates are best suited to the role and which are not ❑
d) They are not usefull at all ❑

3. Which type of interview question have we covered in this chapter?
a) Outcome-based ❑
b) Behavioural ❑
c) Both of the above ❑
d) Neither of the above ❑

4. A first interview would typically last how long?
a) 45–60 minutes ❑
b) 2 hours ❑
c) 10–20 minutes ❑
d) One day ❑

5. It is very important that the interviewer has read the candidate's CV before starting the interview.
a) True ❑
b) False ❑
c) Not sure ❑
d) Makes no difference ❑

6. Which of the following are part of the two-step process in planning interview questions?
a) List the information needed to be found out in the interview ❑
b) Create questions based around this information needed ❑
c) Both of the above ❑
d) Neither of the above ❑

7. In typical circumstances, when selecting candidates for interview it is acceptable to select only candidates who:
a) Are single ❑
b) Have previously worked in a similar job role ❑
c) Are female ❑
d) Are religious ❑

8. How can a recruitment firm help you in the recruitment process?
a) Help select candidates to be interviewed ❑
b) Meet candidates to prepare summaries about each candidate ❑
c) Both of the above ❑
d) Neither of the above ❑

THURSDAY

# How to choose
# the ideal
# candidate

> *'If I were running a company today, I would have one priority above all others: to acquire as many of the best people as I could.'*
>
> Jim Collins

> *'You're only as good as the people you hire.'*
>
> Ray Kroc

This chapter will complete the process of how to select the ideal candidate for your vacancy and will explore a number of important topics including:

- How to keep candidates warm and interested in your role and company
- How to communicate with candidates and how to give them feedback after interviews
- Exploring creative ideas in order to impress candidates to make them keen to join your company
- How you might complement the interviewing process by having candidates take some kinds of behavioural assessments or psychometric tests. You may also check a candidate's skills, for example their English language written ability or their business skills
- How to carry out reference checks, also called employment background checks, to be able to verify the person's employment and education history and to also learn how the candidate performed in any previous roles. You will also learn about checking the individual's name on the internet
- Understanding the candidates' availability in terms of clauses that might exist in their current employment contracts and other factors that might delay them being able to start with your company
- Exploring all the criteria that can be used to rank candidates and to decide which one will be offered the job

# Keeping candidates warm and giving them feedback

Many of us are so busy with our mobile phones, emails and endless meetings that we can often neglect some important tasks.

Job-seekers often complain that they are left in the dark during the recruitment process and are given no feedback. I know of companies that have interviewed a candidate and then forgot to communicate that the candidate had been rejected. Perhaps they did not wish to communicate the bad news, but does keeping quiet in this way help your company's employer branding and reputation?

Giving timely feedback to all candidates is important and today, with the existence of emails, all you have to do is to ensure that candidates receive email notifications, with phone calls when necessary. This is especially important if the recruitment process is slow and candidates are being kept waiting for the next round of interviews.

Whenever possible try to speak with candidates by phone rather than by email. The intention of the phone call may simply be to change an interview time or location, but during a short call you can also build up a positive rapport, asking how things are going.

If you are using a recruitment firm to help fill a job vacancy, ensure that they are told to communicate well with all candidates who have been rejected as well as with all those who are still in what I call the recruitment pipeline, that is, still under consideration.

When you have completed all of your interviews and have chosen the candidate you wish to hire, do not 'put all of your eggs in one basket' and immediately reject all the other candidates. Is there a second or even third choice candidate that you can 'keep warm'?

# Creative ways of impressing candidates

Are you trying to attract candidates who are 'in demand', who your competitors may also wish to hire? Even if you are not sure whether your candidates are 'in demand', I encourage you to consider the following ideas to implement with your candidates, at least for the final two or three candidates:

● Why not invite candidates for lunch or for a drink? Or interview them over a breakfast meeting?
● Walk them around your office or plant and introduce them to people.
● Let them meet their potential colleagues in order to enable them to ask questions and to better understand your company, job role and working culture and so on.
● Above all, make your candidates feel valued and special, by giving them as much time as possible.

# Using assessment tools and centres

During an interview, you can assess the candidate's work experience, education, qualifications, soft skills and competencies, which can help you answer two key questions:

# Is the candidate eligible?

Eligibility is about whether the person can do the job well. Do they have the right technical or hard skills, work experience and so on? This is generally quite easy to measure and judge during an interview process and through reviewing the person's paperwork (certificates, CV, references and so on).

# Is the candidate suitable?

Suitability is asking whether the person will do the job well. This is based on the person's mind-set, personality, soft skills and behaviours. In the interviewing process, I showed you how to try to create questions that will help you to better understand the person's behaviours. But this is not easy to do as you are simply relying upon answers to verbal questions.

A more systematic and scientific way to assess a candidate's behaviours, motivations and personality is to give the candidate some kind of behavioural assessment or psychometric test.

These involve the individual being asked to complete some kind of online questionnaire from which results can be produced. The results of the assessment are a report made up of a mix of table, graphs and commentary that describe aspects of the individual's personality and skills.

You can find many such tests on the web and they typically cost up to US$200 (£150) for one individual. Examples of some commonly used tools include:

● The Harrison Assessment
● Decision Dynamics
● Lifestyle Inventory
● DISC
● MBTI

You might consider using an assessment for a critical job vacancy such as a key managerial position. If you are using a recruitment firm, you could ask them for advice on any assessment tools that they may be able to help you administer.

Many global multinationals such as HSBC, Shell and Macquarie Bank use assessment tools for all, or most, of their external recruiting and they have created templates that help check the degree of fit between the individual and any job role in terms of the soft skills and competencies needed for success in that job.

You might need to administer more than one assessment to your candidates and you may even consider involving trained psychologists in the evaluation of a candidate or of a group of candidates. In such cases, you could be organizing or using some kind of assessment centre. Such centres involve candidates taking a series of assessments, tests and challenges, often while being observed. This is often done by larger organizations for their managerial level of recruitment and may be organized in-house or could be outsourced to a global assessments firm.

## Additional tests

For certain jobs you may also ask candidates to complete certain tests to check their skill levels. Examples might include giving typing or computer skills tests to candidates for a personal assistant job. For other roles, you may give candidates written English language tests, or driving tests.

For professional and managerial job vacancies, companies may give candidates different kinds of tests, activities and assessments. Occasionally, candidates may be asked to prepare a short presentation on a particular topic.

# Carrying out background checks

When you have chosen the final one or two candidates to fill a vacant position, it is good practice to check out their employment history and backgrounds. Such checks can be:

- employment background checks
- education and qualification checks
- internet name searches
- criminal and credit history checks.

## Employment background checks

During the interviewing process you have simply based your conclusions on what the candidate has been telling you, including in the content of their CV. It is good to check the validity of the information and also to explore what any past employers may think of the candidate's work performance.

What exactly is an employer background check? Normally the candidate would name some past colleagues (normally a

boss, senior colleague or Human Resource Manager) as their referees. The referees would be willing to speak to you about the candidate. You would normally speak on the phone or via email with such a referee and could ask them questions such as:

- Could you confirm the period during which X worked for your company?
- In what positions? Who did X report to?
- What were X's responsibilities? How many staff reported to X?
- How would you describe X's performance?
- What was X's working style and people management style like?
- Why did X leave? Would you re-hire X?

Sometimes the referee may not wish to say very much, but if you are able to speak with the referee you can normally get a sense for how they felt about the candidate when they worked together.

Often a referee would write a 'To whom it may concern' reference letter which a candidate would pass you. You could then follow this by speaking with the referee.

In some countries, there are privacy laws and there is also a risk of a referee being sued by a candidate for things the referee may reveal, particularly if the comments were not positive and as a result the new employer does not hire the candidate. As a result, many reference checks simply serve to verify the basic information, for example dates of employment and job title. This does mean that it is hard to learn how a candidate may have performed in past jobs and why a candidate may have left any past employers.

## Education and qualification checks

It is also advisable to consider verifying any key educational qualifications, professional memberships and accreditations. This is essential in certain situations, for example checking a Finance Director candidate's accounting qualifications. In other less important cases, you may be happy to accept photocopies of candidates' certificates and qualifications.

In certain countries, it is quite common for job seekers to lie about their background, education and work experience. I have had plenty of first-hand experience of this in my time as a headhunter.

## Internet name search

In recent years it has become common to carry out searches on the web to see what, if any, presence the individual has on the web and to see what comments they may make or others may have made about them.

You could type the candidate's name into:

- an internet search engine (In addition to conducting a web search, you could also search images and also videos. If the candidate has a common name, you may not find anything about them, but may have more to look at if their name is unusual.)
- social networking sites such as Facebook, Twitter and LinkedIn.

## Criminal and credit history checks

You may also carry out a check of any criminal records and also to check the individual's credit history. Sometimes owners and managers of smaller organizations would not consider such checks but in my opinion it is better to be safe than sorry and to spend a small sum to protect your company from possible large problems in the future.

In most countries, there are companies that you could use to carry out all of the above checks (background, internet, criminal and credit history).

# Understanding the candidates' availability

Imagine that you have worked through a recruitment process and you are left with two finalist candidates, after rejecting all the other candidates for various reasons. You now compare both candidates based on how soon they could join your company:

| Candidates remaining under consideration | How soon could they join your company after accepting a job offer? |
|---|---|
| Candidate A | in 1 month |
| Candidate B | in 5 months |

Based on their availability, which candidate would you rather hire? I suspect Candidate A would win your vote. One month is not long, but five months is a long time in your business. You must remember to check when a candidate could start work with you, and do not leave such a check until the last minute. If a candidate is currently not working – either recently graduated from college, between jobs or unemployed – they could start work with you immediately upon being given a letter of employment. This would be a plus point for such candidates. This will not be the case with candidates who are currently working.

Early in the interview process, you should ask all candidates about their potential availability by asking about their:

- contractual notice period
- any untaken annual holiday leave
- any garden leave clauses
- any non-compete clauses
- any upcoming bonus payments or share option redemptions.

Let us explore each of these:

## Notice period

Most employees would have a notice period in their employment contract, which may vary from one week to as long as six months, or potentially for very senior roles even longer. If the notice period is long, might the candidate be able to buy out all or part by paying their employer an 'in-lieu of notice' payment?

## Untaken leave

Could any untaken annual leave be offset against the notice period so that the notice period is reduced?

## Garden leave clause

Does the candidate have a restriction in the employment contract that, for a period of time after resigning, the individual must serve a notice period as paid leave during which time they would not be able to work for a new employer?

## Non-compete clauses

If you are trying to recruit a candidate who is working with one of your competitors, do check whether the candidate's employment contract has a non-compete clause stating that for a period of time, which is normally 12 months, they cannot work for a competitor. You may wish to help the candidate to check whether such a clause is legally enforceable.

## Bonus and share options

Is the candidate awaiting a bonus payment (e.g. at the year end), vesting of share options or other rewards and would they be reluctant to resign from their employer before receiving such payments? In the next chapter, we discuss how to negotiate remuneration and will discuss whether you might have to consider compensating for such a lost bonus in return for the candidate joining you sooner.

## Obtaining a work visa

If the candidate needs a work visa or permit to be able to work in your country, how long will this take? Are you willing to wait so long? And who will pay the cost of the visa process?

## Other reasons delaying a candidate's possible departure

Humans are quite loyal, even Generation Y, and you will be surprised how reluctant people can be to resign immediately. They may wish to finish a project, or wait for their boss to come back from medical leave. The list of possible excuses is quite long.

Are the candidate's spouse, partner and/or any other key family members supportive of the candidate potentially joining your company? Sometimes, you might be surprised where resistance may come from.

Do get to know your candidate well in order to understand how willing they would be to resign once you have made them an offer.

# Ranking candidates for a job offer

For those candidates selected for interview, the following checklist summarises the selection process to date:

| Checklist | Comments or scores |
| --- | --- |
| CV – work experience, education, qualifications | |
| First interview | |
| Second interview | |
| Later interviews | |
| Assessment tool and other test results | |
| Reference tool results | |
| Other background check results | |
| Availability to start work | |
| Remuneration expectations | |
| Other factors (e.g. willingness to relocate) | |

Note: Remuneration expectations will be covered in the next chapter when we explore how to negotiate with a candidate. How are you going to decide who is offered the job? What is the process? Here are some helpful questions to ask yourself:

● Are you the sole decision-maker? Or does it involve a few of you?
● Is there a formal sign-off or approvals process or is it simply requiring a verbal 'Go ahead and hire them?

Do you consider hiring a candidate who:

● might be a little under-qualified but could grow into the job role
● is potentially over-experienced for the role, but could fill the role very well (but will they stay long if you are not able to offer them something larger)?

You need to decide what factors are important in choosing between candidates. Would you reject an otherwise strong candidate for reasons such as:

● having too high salary expectations
● not being available to join the company within one month

- having a poor behavioural assessment result
- having poor references

Will you keep a second candidate warm (see the next chapter on this topic)?

The recruitment process can be made systematic and somewhat scientific, but the final decision about who you will choose to hire is an art and not a science. Being a good manager or leader is about learning how to make such choices.

# Be ready to start the search again

It is sometimes the right decision to not hire a candidate.

Do not to be desperate and hire a candidate who may be the 'least bad' of all the candidates. In my experience, it is better to seek more candidates and to delay the recruitment process than to hire a candidate who may not even successfully pass your probation period. There may be rare exceptions to this, for example if the business truly cannot function if the job role is not filled.

If you have been using a recruitment firm to help you to find and source candidates, they will not be happy if you inform them that you have rejected all the candidates and that you need a new batch of candidates to select from. The recruitment firm consultant may push back by:

- claiming that there are no more suitable candidates – I would urge you stick to what you believe as it is you who has to work with the chosen candidate
- trying to talk you into reconsidering any of the current pool of finalist candidates. In my opinion, this is nonsense and in 99 per cent of cases there are always more possible candidates out there, but it does take effort to find them – more advertising, cold-calling and/or looking again through databases
- seeking a higher fee for the extra work involved. I would urge you to only agree to pay for any extra disbursement costs, for example cost of any new job advertisements.

# Summary

After working through this chapter you will now be able to professionally and effectively choose which candidate you wish to offer a job to.

● You now understand the importance of keeping candidates warm and of giving them timely and personal feedback. In addition you are now aware of creative ways in which you can keep candidates interested and impressed in your company – of how to make them feel important.

● You will now be able to consider giving candidates a behavioural assessment or psychometric test or even to arrange attendance at a more comprehensive assessment centre. And we also explained that some companies may give a variety of other tests to candidates, such as written English tests or a computer skills test.

● We have explored the important area of carrying out a variety of background checks covering a candidate's employment, criminal, credit and internet presence histories.

- We have also covered the issue of candidate availability and of the reasons why a candidate may not be able to join your company immediately.

- Finally, we explored how you will decide which candidate will be offered the job, noting that no matter how systematic your recruitment process is, it is not easy deciding which candidate can best fit into your job role and sometimes there may not be a suitable candidate.

# Questions (answers at the back)

1. Why would you use a behavioural assessment tool?
a) To test someone's English ability ❑
b) To assess a candidate's soft skills and competencies ❑
c) To check someone's employment history ❑
d) To verify someone's salary ❑

2. When might you have to find more candidates?
a) When you have more job roles to fill ❑
b) When none of the existing candidates are suitable ❑
c) Both of the above ❑
d) None of the above ❑

3. Background checks are not normally carried out on:
a) Family history ❑
b) Employment history ❑
c) Credit history ❑
d) Past work performance ❑

4. What is a referee?
a) Someone who interviews the candidate ❑
b) Someone who provides a reference ❑
c) Someone who writes the job description ❑
d) The interviewer ❑

5. All else being equal, which candidate would normally be preferred?
a) A candidate who can start work with your company in four months ❑
b) A candidate who can start work with your company immediately ❑

c) A candidate who can start work with your company in one month ❑
d) A candidate who has no interest in your company ❑

6. To keep a candidate warm it is better to:
a) Email them ❑
b) Write them a letter ❑
c) Telephone them ❑
d) Ignore them ❑

7. Harrison and the MBTI are examples of what?
a) Behavioural assessment tools ❑
b) Companies that carry out background checks ❑
c) Interviewing styles ❑
d) Job websites ❑

8. Which of the following is NOT a reason a candidate may not be able to immediately start work with you?
a) Garden leave clause ❑
b) Notice period ❑
c) Probation period ❑
d) Until they have completed a medical ❑

9. A non-compete clause prohibits someone from working:
a) For their employer ❑
b) For a competitor ❑
c) Overtime ❑
d) At weekends ❑

10. 'Suitability' assesses whether a candidate:
a) Can do the job ❑
b) Will do the job ❑
c) Neither of the above ❑
d) Both of the above ❑

# FRIDAY

**Ensuring that your chosen candidate accepts your job offer**

> *'Development can help great people be even better – but if I had a dollar to spend, I'd spend 70 cents getting the right person in the door.'*
>
> Paul Russell, Director, Leadership and Development, Google

Having chosen which candidate you wish to hire, you now need to create and make a job offer and to have the candidate accept your job offer. This can be a tricky process and is sometimes referred to as helping a candidate to 'cross the line'.

This chapter will walk you through this process, sharing with you all the key milestones and issues you may need to address, including:

- Determining when you will make the offer, either before or after all the background checks have been completed
- Helping you think through the most important part of this stage of the recruitment process, which is deciding what you offer the candidate, including focussing on the main part of any job offer: the remuneration package
- Understanding how and why you may need to obtain past salary verification information, as well also exploring how you might obtain market salary information to help you assess whether a planned remuneration offer will be competitive
- How to create and share a verbal offer, a job offer and an employment contract
- Working through the negotiation process, including facing counter offers from the candidate's current employer
- The pros and cons of having a recruitment firm help you through this part of the recruitment process

# Timing of a job offer

When should you give a candidate an offer of employment, or what can also be called a job offer? You may give or make an offer of employment after all background and reference checks have been completed or you may give an offer beforehand that states it is subject to any such checks being satisfactory.

# What will you offer?

On Tuesday, we explored the topic of attracting candidates and maximizing your employer branding. This marketing or branding focussed work will have helped you to attract candidates to apply for a job vacancy, but once you arrive at the point of wishing to hire a particular candidate you will need to decide what exactly you offer the candidate.

## Remuneration

*'If you pick the right people and give them the opportunity to spread their wings – and put compensation as a carrier behind it – you almost don't have to manage them.'*

Jack Welch

Remuneration is normally viewed as the most important part of any job offer.

Remuneration can also be called the salary, salary package, earnings, wages or income. All these terms refer to how much a person is paid. When hiring a candidate, it is normally discussed in terms of an annual remuneration package made up of:

● base guaranteed salary
● discretionary bonuses and commissions

- other monetary benefits such as travel allowances, share options, company car, club memberships and medical insurance
- non-monetary benefits such as holiday entitlements.

The question of what level of remuneration you should offer a candidate can be a difficult one. Some of the issues to consider might include:

- Do you have a fixed grading and salary structure?
- Do you have any flexibility in what you can offer? Do you need to get approval from others in your organization?
- Will a candidate move to a new company for the same salary? How much do you have to offer to attract them?
- What are the current market levels of remuneration?
- With young recent graduates looking for a new job, do you have to offer more than other companies to attract them?
- What is the candidate's most recent salary package?
- What are the candidate's expectations?
- Are there any specific things that a particular candidate needs to be offered to have them accept an offer?

### Past salary verification

If the candidate is requesting a level of salary that is higher than your planned budget, you may wish to ask the candidate, directly or via a recruitment firm consultant, to provide some verification or proof of their most recent salary package.

Some organizations make salary verification a mandatory part of their background reference checking process for all newly hired employees.

How would you react if you discovered that a candidate has lied and exaggerated about their existing remuneration package? In my experience, this is more common than one might imagine.

### Are your remuneration packages competitive?

I would encourage you to reflect upon the following questions:

- Have you had trouble hiring staff in the past?

- Have candidates ever declined to accept job offers that you have made them?
- Did they tell you what parts of the offer they found unattractive or were they declining for other reasons?
- Have you had many newly hired staff leave your company?
- Were you able to talk to them to ask why they were choosing to leave, in what are called exit interviews?

**Market level of remuneration**

You could seek information about the level of salaries that are being paid for similar job roles in the same or related industries in your city, county or even country. This can help you to assess the competitiveness of your company's remuneration levels.

Where can you obtain such information? You might be able to informally gather such salary data through speaking with some other companies or through your local Chamber of Commerce. Alternatively, if you have the available expense budget you could pay for professional advice. Such professional salary survey data is needed when you are a larger organization and are needing to hire a large number of people (e.g. as part of creating a new division) or if you are creating a totally new position and you have no history of how much to pay to attract someone.

# The job offer and an employment contract

There are a few ways of giving someone a job offer, and in certain countries there may be differences but as a rule there are three key ways in which a company can extend an offer to a candidate:

- with a verbal offer
- by giving a job offer letter
- by creating an employment contract

Employers often start the employment offer process by giving verbal offers. Such an offer could be given over the phone, in person or via a recruitment firm consultant. It could be as simple as saying 'We would like to offer you the job...' or it may include verbally sharing all the key parts of the job offer including the remuneration details. It is very important that you follow through with such verbal offers and that any follow-up written offers should be aligned with the verbal offer.

Larger organizations may have the benefit a well-established Human Resources department, in-house legal staff and the experience of having drafted many employment contracts.

Hiring managers at smaller organizations may have to draft the paperwork themselves. In such cases, it is important to be aware of any relevant employment, work or labour legislation and laws when drafting such employment paperwork. If you are ever in this situation, I would recommend that you seek the advice of a lawyer or some other employment contract specialist.

What should you include in a job offer and employment contract? Rules vary by country and by company. The following headings are typically included in any employment contract with the key parts possibly being included in a separate offer letter and/or in a verbal offer. I have added some comments for you to consider.

- **Job title** – is this the same as the title shown in any job advertisements and shared during the interviews?
- **Reporting line** – to whom does the role report?
- **Start date** – a date should be given, which would hopefully be a verbally and mutually agreed date, and it should not come as a shock to the candidate
- **Remuneration details**
- **Annual base salary** – giving details of when it will be paid, for example payable in 12 equal parts on the last day of each month
- **Bonus/commission details**
- **Probation period** – will the candidate be given a period of probation? The next chapter will explore this in more detail

- **Notice period** – how many weeks or months of notice should either party give the other? This is normally shorter during the probation period
- **Work location** – will they be based in your office or plant or can they work from home?
- **Working hours** – are your company's working hours standard or are they flexible? Has the candidate already been warned that you work on Saturday mornings or that the working day starts at 7.30 a.m.?
- **Job responsibilities and duties** – a summary may be given in a job offer letter or employment contract. Alternatively a job description could be attached as an appendix
- **Any allowances or expenses policies** – for example, for travel
- **Holidays** – what will you offer beyond any minimum statutory levels? Would you match the holiday entitlement of the candidate's previous role?
- **Confidentiality clause** – this would be intended to prevent an employee from revealing confidential company information to third parties
- **Non-compete or garden clause** – in the previous chapter, we explored what happens if the candidate has such clauses in their existing employment contract. Will you also include some kind of restriction clauses in your employment contract?
- **Company or human resource policies** – there might be a section which refers to employment related policies contained in a separate document or handbook (see the section below)
- **'Subject to' clause** – the offer of employment might be subject to the company obtaining satisfactory employment background checks, education and qualification checks, criminal and credit history checks and/or a medical examination
- **Acceptance section** – this would be an area at the bottom of the offer letter or employment contract for the candidate to sign and date

# Employee or HR handbook

Are many of your standard terms and conditions of employment contained in some kind of employee handbook or HR handbook? Is this updated regularly and are the terms contained within it attractive and competitive? Ideally it should be reviewed annually, particularly if there are any changes to the labour or employment legislation and laws in your country.

Ideally, you should give candidates a copy of your most updated handbook when you pass the candidate the job offer. If you only let them see a copy of the handbook when they join your company, they may learn of policies which they do not like and had they known of them earlier they may have chosen not to join your company.

# Negotiation process

Nothing in an offer of employment should surprise the candidate – in an ideal world you would have shared your key working practices and employment conditions with the candidate during the interview process.

You may be fortunate and find that your candidate will accept your employment offer without any questions, push back or negotiation. This tends to happen when you have either:

- an unemployed candidate who is desperate to re-enter the workforce and is afraid to question or complain about anything you offer for fear of you taking back the offer
- a young recently graduated candidate who has no experience of job offers and is simply eager to start work.

You should work on the assumption that your candidate will raise questions and may wish to negotiate on various parts of the job offer. If the candidate is happily working in a job and has come to you through an executive search or headhunting process, they could be quite demanding, telling your executive search consultant or you directly that they will move only if they are offered certain things.

## Dealing with counter offers from a candidate's current employer

Think about this scenario:

Imagine that you have a candidate, who is currently working, to whom you give a verbal or written job offer.

The candidate accepts your offer and now needs to resign from a current job.

The candidate comes back to you in writing or verbally saying: *'My current employer does not want me to resign and they are willing to increase my base salary by 20 per cent and they promise to raise my job description to a manager level by the end of the year. This is better than what you are offering me.'*

Such scenarios are very common particularly for key job positions where a company cannot face the prospect of losing a key person. But sometimes it could just be a ploy by a candidate to negotiate improved terms of a job offer.

What should you do? Do you negotiate to try to have the candidate accept your job offer or do you walk away, telling the candidate that the terms of the job offer are the best that you can offer and cannot be changed?

In my experience, the key decision-making criteria is: how badly do you wish to hire this candidate? Do you have other back-up candidates? Have you time to seek more candidates?

# Having a recruitment firm help with the offer and negotiation process

If you have been using a recruitment firm to help you with the recruitment process to date, you must decide how you involve the firm's contact person (normally a recruitment consultant or partner) in the process of making a candidate an offer and having the candidate accept. There are three options:

- Do not involve the recruitment firm at all, and communicate directly with the candidate on all matters.
- Work through the recruitment firm to pass all communications between your company and the candidate.
- Work with the recruitment firm, but have some direct communication with the candidate.

There are pros and cons of working through a recruitment firm. On the positive side, the recruitment firm:

- can help with any difficult or tricky discussions, with the candidate possibly feeling more comfortable sharing any concerns through such a third party
- is used to helping companies make offers to candidates, and then dealing with the follow-up issues
- has an incentive to have the candidate accept the employment offer given that all or part of their fee would only be payable once a candidate has started work with you.

## What are the downsides of working through a recruitment firm?

If the firm's fee is based on a percentage of the candidate's first-year salary package, then the recruitment firm's staff might try to inflate the level of salary that you must offer to attract the candidate. This could be through them coaching the candidate on what to ask for or simply telling you directly what the candidate's salary expectations are.

They might push a candidate to accept a job offer from you by misrepresenting what it is you that are offering in terms of the job opportunity and benefits. As a result, you may have a candidate joining your company but not staying very long – this will be explored in more detail in the next chapter.

# Summary

After working through this chapter, you are now able to hire a candidate and work with them to sign an employment contract with your company:

● You have an understanding of when you will give a candidate a job offer, timing it to be given before or after any background checks.

● We have explored in detail what exactly you will offer a candidate, including the key topic of what salary or remuneration package you will offer. You should remember that you can seek proof of the candidate's current salary as well as reviewing the market levels of salary.

● We have walked you through how to create a job offer and how it can be given verbally and through a detailed employment contract accompanied with an employee or HR handbook.

● We then explored the important issue of the negotiating the job offer with a candidate and dealing with the situation of a candidate's current employer making a counter offer.

SUNDAY
MONDAY
TUESDAY
WEDNESDAY
THURSDAY
FRIDAY
SATURDAY

- The pros and cons of involving a recruitment firm in the negotiation were also explained, giving you enough insight to decide whether you would use a recruitment firm at this point of the recruitment.

- You are now ready to welcome the candidate on board in your company as a new employee. In the next and final chapter of this book, we will explore how you can ensure that your recruitment is a success as measured by having a new employee join your company who then stays and performs well in their role.

# Questions (answers at the back)

1. When is it possible to give a candidate a job offer?
   - a) Before completing the background and reference checks ❏
   - b) After completing the background and reference checks ❏
   - c) Either before or after completing the background and reference checks ❏
   - d) Before the candidate has been interviewed ❏

2. Why verify a candidate's past salary details?
   - a) To check that the candidate has been honest ❏
   - b) To assess whether your planned remuneration offer will be attractive to the candidate ❏
   - c) Both of the above ❏
   - d) None of the above ❏

3. Which of the following is not normally included in remuneration?
   - a) Base salary ❏
   - b) Working hours ❏
   - c) Bonus payments ❏
   - d) Age of the candidate ❏

4. Which types of candidates will often accept a job offer without negotiating?
   - a) Unemployed candidates ❏
   - b) Recently graduated candidates ❏
   - c) Both of the above ❏
   - d) None of the above ❏

5. If a candidate's current employer tries to keep them by making an improved offer, should you negotiate and increase the terms of your job offer?
   - a) Sometimes ❏
   - b) Never ❏
   - c) Always ❏
   - d) Not sure ❏

6. Having a recruitment firm help you with any remuneration negotiation is:
   - a) A good idea ❏
   - b) Not a good idea ❏
   - c) Sometimes helpful ❏
   - d) Not sure ❏

7. An employment contract does not include which of the following:
   - a) CV of the candidate ❏
   - b) Job title ❏
   - c) Working hours ❏
   - d) Salary offer ❏

8. The 'Subject to' clause in an employment contract normally refers to:
   - a) The background checks ❏
   - b) End of probation period ❏
   - c) Interviewing process ❏
   - d) Time of day ❏

9. An employee or HR handbook is normally:
   - a) Never shown to the candidate ❏
   - b) Given to the candidate when you make a job offer ❏
   - c) Given to the candidate when they come for a first interview ❏
   - d) Ignored ❏

# SATURDAY

**Transforming a candidate into a successful employee**

> *'People are definitely a company's greatest asset. It doesn't make any difference whether the product is cars or cosmetics. A company is only as good as the people it keeps.'*
>
> Mary Kay Ash

This final chapter will share with you how to ensure that your newly hired candidate can become a successful employee. A recruitment process can only be called a true success if a candidate joins and stays with your company and becomes a happy and productive employee.

We will explore what you can do between the day a candidate accepts a job offer and the day that they start work with your company.

We then explore the issue of expectations showing how easily a candidate can join you as a new employee full of many expectations and then there can quickly and easily arise a mismatch of expectations, which can lead to the new employee leaving your company. There are ways of avoiding this.

The candidate's first few days and weeks working in the new role are critical in determining whether your new employee will be successful and will stay with your organization. This initial period can be viewed as the same period as any contractual probation period.

Finally, we will discuss how you can measure the effectiveness of a recruitment process through exploring a number of different recruitment measures or metrics that you could adopt.

# The candidate has accepted your job offer – mission completed?

When a candidate has accepted an employment offer or an employment contract, you might think that the recruitment process is completed. No, it is not! You still need to ensure that the candidate comes to work on day one and, more importantly, comes to work and performs well during their probation period.

If your candidate is immediately available and you are ready to have them start working with you then the gap between them accepting a job offer and commencing work might be less than one day.

However, as we discussed on Thursday, your candidate may have with their existing employer a long notice period or even a period of garden leave or a period when they cannot work for a competitor. As a result, you could have to wait a few months for your candidate to be able to start working with you.

You might try reducing this 'waiting period' through encouraging the candidate to negotiate with the existing employer. You could offer to compensate the candidate if he or she is able to buy out of any notice period clauses. It would typically be one month's salary for every month of notice period, often called 'in lieu of notice period'.

If you have to wait for your candidate, what should you do during this period? From my experience, you need to do something to help counter any the following potential issues.

Here is my advice:

- The candidate may have trouble resigning. It is good to talk with the candidate about how and when they will resign from their current job.
- The candidate may have second thoughts and change their mind about wishing to join your company – this could be for any number of reasons.
- The candidate may receive other job offers and may decide to turn down your offer of employment, even if he has signed an acceptance.

What can you do to counter these risks? There are a few things that you could consider, including:

- Keep in close and regular contact with the candidate. Speak on the phone once every one or two weeks and possibly meet up for lunch.
- Involve the candidate in the business – invite them to attend one or two meetings. It is particularly good if you are having any offsite or weekend meetings that you could invite them to.
- Give the candidate materials to read and even seek the advice of the candidate on one or two business issues.
- Above all, you need to engage with and excite the candidate about what you and your colleagues are doing and make it harder for the candidate to back out during this waiting period.

One of the benefits of hiring a candidate who is unemployed is that they will not have the need to resign nor will they have an employer trying to retain them.

If you are unlucky enough to lose a candidate after they have accepted your job offer, you may have to start the search for candidates all over again.

# What are your candidate's expectations?

When a candidate does start work in a new job, a cause of potential concern or difficulty can arise from the candidate experiencing things and situations that they were not expecting.

When I was a headhunter, I would sometimes have a candidate call me after only a few days in the job to say that they were not happy and their reasoning would nearly always start with the statement 'I was not expecting...' or 'I did not realize...' Examples might include:

- 'I was not expecting to have to work such long hours...'
- 'I was not expecting to have such a small workspace...'
- 'I never realized that I would have so much tedious work...'
- 'I never expected my boss to be so hard to work with and he never seems to listen to what I have to say...'

## Aligning expectations

In the diagram below, you see that a new employee would have expectations of what they expect to give as well as expectations of what they expect to receive from their employer; and likewise, the employer would have expectations of what they would expect to give to and to receive from the new employee.

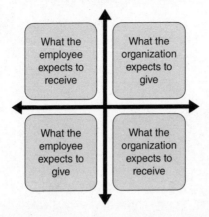

The ideal solution is that during the interviewing process you try to share as much information as possible with the candidates so that when the chosen candidate starts work with you, your expectations will be aligned with theirs.

Taking the above three complaints by the candidate as examples, during the interview process you would hope that:

- the candidate would fully understand what the real working hours are
- the candidate would have been shown the workspace
- you would have tried to explain and show the kind of work that the candidate would have to do, including the not so exciting parts.

Ensure that the candidate meets with and spends time with their new boss to better understand their working style and expectations. This may involve more than just having a one hour interview with them.

# The candidate's first few weeks at work

The first day is very important and you should realize that not every employee will come back to work on the second day

– a study by the UK recruitment firm Reed found that 4 per cent of new employees leave their new job on the first day of employment.

During the new employee's first day at work, you should try to make sure that you meet with the individual, asking:

- 'Is everything turning out as you expected?'
- 'Is there anything which surprises or upsets you?'

## Induction programme

A structured way of trying to make sure that a new employee's first few weeks and months are successful is to create a structured programme of sharing and support.

If your company does not have anything in place, it is quite easy to create such a programme, even for a small company that may have only one or two new hires each year. What should the programme include?

### Welcome pack

You could give them a welcome pack and walk them through it. The welcome pack might include:

- details about the company's mission and vision statements, core values
- copies of a recent annual report
- details of how to use the company's IT systems, including any intranet, websites, email systems, online address book and so on
- various policies, including expenses.

### Getting equipped

Make sure that the new member of staff is given an organizer, phone, computer, company car and so on, make sure that their email account is set up, and that they settle into their work station or office.

### Tour and introductions

Give the individual tours and allow them to meet their colleagues.

### One-on-one sharing

The employee's boss, colleagues and/or a mentor should be encouraged to spend time explaining the company's work habits, informal networks and working culture.

### Give the new employee your time

This is the most important part of any induction or onboarding programme.

Listen well to what they are saying and also to what others are saying about the new employee.

Change is not easy and starting a new job is a major example of change for any person to have to go through. Understand that they may miss things that they became used to in their previous job or during their recent student life.

### How long should an induction programme last?

I would suggest that the programme should last for at least as long as the probation period (which we explore below).

It should never really stop and all employees should be given support and help but as a rule of thumb a formal programme would last only up to 100 days.

# Probation period

Typically the probation period lasts:

● one month for non-managerial roles
● three months for managerial and director level positions.

Why might you give a candidate, in their employment offer, a probation period? During the probation period, the notice period is shorter than it would be after probation. A common example would be a one week notice period during probation and a one month notice period after probation is completed.

When a new employee has successfully completed a probation period with your company, I would suggest that only at that point can you claim that the recruitment has been a success.

This concludes our explanation of how you can conduct a recruitment process from the initial planning phase up to the candidate successfully passing their probation period. We now conclude this chapter with a discussion of how you can measure the success of the entire recruitment process.

## Recruitment metrics

There is the adage: *You can only improve what you can measure.*

Many companies have become scientific in measuring the productivity and effectiveness of their recruitment processes, assessing and setting targets for such measures or metrics as:

● number of applicants received per dollar or pound spent
● time taken by a recruitment firm to supply candidates
● number of candidates interviewed from a sourcing channel
● time taken to complete the recruitment process
● cost of filling a job vacancy.

I would encourage you to copy some of these metrics and monitor your own company's time, money and other resources that are invested in the recruitment process.

# Summary

This final chapter has completed the entire recruitment process or what is sometimes called the pipeline.

● You have ideas of how to keep a candidate warm during the waiting period from when the candidate accepts your job offer until they start work with you.

● You now realize that a candidate accepting a job offer is not the end of the process and only once a candidate has started work and successfully passed their probation period can your recruitment for that particular job vacancy be viewed as complete.

● You also understand the issue of aligning expectations and of helping the candidate succeed through the probation period with a structured induction programme. And you now understand how you measure the effectiveness and efficiency of your recruitment process.

In truth, recruitment for an organization never finishes and you should always be on the lookout for talent that your company could consider hiring.

SUNDAY

MONDAY

TUESDAY

WEDNESDAY

THURSDAY

FRIDAY

SATURDAY

I wish you well in all of your recruitment endeavours and I leave you with the words of Michael Dell, the founder of Dell:

*'The ability to find and hire the right people can make or break your business. It is as plain as that. No matter where you are in the life cycle of your business, bringing in great talent should always be a top priority.'*

# Questions (answers at the back)

1. An induction programme could include which of the following:
a) Welcome pack ❑
b) One-on-one sharing ❑
c) Both of the above ❑
d) None of the above ❑

2. How many sets of expectations are there between a candidate starting a new job and their employer?
a) 2 ❑
b) 4 ❑
c) 1 ❑
d) 12 ❑

3. Recruitment measures or metrics might include which of the following:
a) Cost per candidate recruited ❑
b) Applicants received per advert placed ❑
c) Both of the above ❑
d) Neither of the above ❑

4. How long does a probation period typically last for?
a) 1–3 months ❑
b) 3–9 months ❑
c) 1 year ❑
d) 10 years ❑

5. During a candidate's first day of work, which question should you ask the newly hired candidate?
a) 'Is everything turning out as you expected?' ❑
b) 'Is there anything which surprises or upsets you?' ❑
c) Both of the above ❑
d) You should not speak with the candidate ❑

6. During the period that you are waiting for the candidate to start work with your company, what is the potential risk or problem that might occur?
a) The candidate spends time with you and your colleagues ❑
b) The candidate changes their mind and turns down the job offer ❑
c) The candidate starts work with you earlier than expected ❑
d) The candidate forgets that you have made them a job offer ❑

7. An induction programme can also be called a:
a) Probation period ❑
b) Onboarding programme ❑
c) Both of the above ❑
d) None of the above ❑

8. A welcome pack might include:
a) An annual evaluation form ❑
b) Candidate's CV ❑
c) Details of staff policies and rules ❑
d) Details of the weather ❑

9. Why is it helpful to align the expectations between the newly hired candidate and the company?
a) To ensure that any misalignment does not arise that may lead to the newly employed candidate failing to succeed ❑
b) To help produce an employee handbook ❑
c) To help attract more applicants for the job role ❑
d) To reduce the time needed for interviewing ❑

# 7 × 7

## 1 Seven essential must-do's to ensure you win the 'war for talent'

● Seek to hire internally before looking externally. Promoting an existing member of your organization is a motivational and cost-effective way to fill a vacancy.

● Always be cost-effective in your recruiting. As an example, before paying high fees to advertise job openings, check first if there are lower-cost avenues available.

● Make good use of linkedin.com and sign up to be a premium user so that you can market your organization effectively and have full access to the database of candidates.

● Ensure that your 'employer branding' is optimal and that people want to work for your organization; ask yourself 'if not, why not?'

● Automate your recruitment process making optimal use of IT, including of the web, the Cloud and also explore Recruitment Process Outsourcing (RPO) solutions.

● If you do not find an excellent candidate first time around, then recommence the recruitment process (very quickly if needed!) – do not settle for second best unless you really have no time!

● Ensure that everyone you hire stays during and beyond their probation periods and regularly check in with them to make sure they are happy working in your organization.

## 2 Seven essential resources to help you succeed in recruiting talent

● *The Professional Recruiter's Handbook: Delivering Excellence in Recruitment Practice* by Jane Newell Brown (Kogan Page,

2012). This book builds on what you have learned in this *In a Week* book and deepens your knowledge.

- www.recruiter.co.uk is a comprehensive website sharing best practice and tips for anyone working as a recruiter (within organizations or for recruitment companies).

- *Thank You for Arguing: What Aristotle, Lincoln, and Homer Simpson Can Teach Us About the Art of Persuasion* by Jay Heinrichs (Three Rivers Press, 2013). A good recruiter has to successfully persuade good candidates to want to join your organization.

- *Influence: The Psychology of Persuasion* by Robert Cialdini (HarperBusiness, 2007). Good candidates will have other job offers and this book helps you learn how to influence people to choose what you have to offer.

- Any up-to-date salary survey that covers or is relevant to your industry, region and/or sector. It is essential that your employment offer letters to candidates are competitive and that you know what your competitors are paying their staff.

- *The 7 Hidden Reasons Employees Leave* by Leigh Branham (Amacom, 2012). This US best-selling book is an important reminder about why people leave a company, often after only one day in a new job. It is a book about what you must not do!

- *The Definitive Book of Body Language* by Allan and Barbara Pease (Orion, 2006). If you are going to spend many hours speaking with and meeting lots of job-seekers then you must understand the basics of body language so that you can better understand each person that you meet.

# 3 Seven key questions to ask anyone you are trying to recruit

(Ask these questions at appropriate times during the recruitment process and once the person has joined you.)

- Why would you like to work with us in this organization?

- What most interests and excites you about this job opportunity?
- What most concerns or worries you about this job opportunity?
- If you join us, how long do you imagine staying?
- Why did you accept this job? (*if you offered them the job*)
- Why did you choose to not accept this job opportunity? (*if they turned down a job offer from you*)
- How could we improve our recruitment process? (*ask at the conclusion of a candidate's recruitment process with you*)

# 4 The seven deadly sins of recruiting talent – things to avoid doing

- Not having clear agreement on what the job description is and the reasons for filling a job opening.
- Rejecting good candidates who are stronger than you are – this is a common mistake made by leaders who are recruiting talent into their own team.
- Judging candidates on first looks and being blind to their strengths.
- Hiring the first candidate who fulfills your criteria and ignoring other strong candidates.
- Discriminating in an illegal way when selecting candidates, e.g. be careful thinking that a certain job must be filled by a man or by a young person etc.
- Rejecting a candidate because they do not accept your initial salary offer – good candidates who value themselves should be expected to challenge if they think an offer is too low.
- Forgetting that a candidate is starting work with you and not giving them a good welcome on their first day of work.

# 5 Seven great business leaders who recruit talent very well

Learn from them by reading their books or researching on the web about their ideas and lives.

- **James Caan**: The British entrepreneur and television host of BBC's *Dragon's Den* has created and sold a very large and successful recruitment company and many of his books contain great insights about how to successfully attract and hire great talent.

- **Dame Anita Roddick**: The British founder of the Body Shop retail group once famously said: 'If you think you're too small to have an impact, try going to bed with a mosquito.' She built up a retail empire starting from a single struggling shop through hiring and then training great talent based around some clearly defined and heart-felt values.

- **Mark Zuckerberg**: The American founder and CEO of Facebook has hired many great staff but his diamond hire was to poach from Google, to be his #2, **Sheryl Sandberg** who has written a great book called *Lean In* (WH Allen, 2013) in which she talks about her own journey. In hiring Sheryl, Mark has a deputy whose skills complement his own, and who is, in many ways, much better than he is.

- **Sheikh Mohammed**: The ruler of Dubai and Vice President of the UAE, has an incredible talent for spotting and placing great talent to lead and run the different government organizations throughout Dubai.

- **Jack Welch**: The American former head of General Electric (GE) which is one of the world's largest companies. Jack spent a lot of time choosing and hiring the right people for senior roles in GE and his former Head of Human Resources, Bill Conaty, wrote about Jack's recruiting style in his book *The Talent Masters* (Random House Business, 2011) which is a must read.

- **Richard DeVos**: US businessman and co-founder of Amway, the world's largest multi-level marketing company. Richard realized early in his business career that a manager or leader's most important task was to recruit really well.

- **Jack Ma**: The Chinese billionaire and founder of the world's largest online buying and selling website, Alibaba, is often called the Steve Jobs of China. Jack is well known for hiring great talent and for admitting when he has made a hiring mistake.

# 6 Seven key recruitment-related quotations

- 'If you pick the right people and give them the opportunity to spread their wings and put compensation as a carrier behind it, you almost don't have to manage them.' Jack Welch, the former CEO of the large US multinational, General Electric

- 'I hire people brighter than me and I get out of their way.' Lee Iacocca, the former CEO of the vehicle manufacturer, Chrysler

- 'The competition to hire the best will increase in the years ahead. Companies that give extra flexibility to their employees will have the edge in this area.' Bill Gates, the billionaire philanthropist and co-founder of the technology group, Microsoft

- 'The secret of my success is that we have gone to exceptional lengths to hire the best people in the world.' Steve Jobs, the co-founder of Apple, one of the world's most profitable companies

- 'A company should limit its growth based on its ability to attract enough of the right people.' Jim Collins, best-selling author of *Good to Great* (Random House Business, 2001)

- 'If you can hire people whose passion intersects with the job, they won't require any supervision at all. They will manage themselves better than anyone could ever manage them. Their fire comes from within, not from without. Their motivation is internal, not external.' Stephen Covey, the leadership guru and best-selling author of *The 7 Habits of Highly Effective People* (Simon & Schuster, 2004)

● 'Never hire someone who knows less than you do about what he's hired to do.' Malcolm Forbes

# 7 Seven essential lists (that form part of any best practice recruitment process)

● List of the decision-makers who will be involved in the recruitment process (e.g. defining the job role, interviewing candidates, creating a candidate's offer letter etc.).

● List of key success criteria – these are those criteria that successful candidates must possess if they are to be considered as strong candidates.

● List of the timeframes that different parts of the recruitment process must follow. So often there is time pressure to fill a job vacancy and good planning involves agreeing up front how much time is available for each part of the process.

● List of short-listed candidates showing how they are ranked based on how well they meet any defined success criteria.

● List of recruitment companies that your organization and industry views as very good. These might be a combination of executive search (headhunting) firms as well as personnel agencies.

● List of those recruitment and job-hunting websites which might be used to post job openings on and to also search for candidates on.

● List of the reasons why candidates turn down job offers and/or remove themselves from a recruitment process. Just as organizations conduct exit interviews when employees leave you, it also wise to do the same for candidates.

# Answers

**Sunday:** 1b; 2b; 3c; 4c; 5b; 6a;
7a; 8c.

**Monday:** 1a; 2b; 3a; 4c; 5b; 6b;
7a; 8b; 9c.

**Tuesday:** 1a; 2b; 3a; 4c; 5b; 6c;
7a; 8b; 9a.

**Wednesday:** 1b; 2c; 3c; 4a; 5a;
6c; 7b; 8c.

**Thursday:** 1b; 2c; 3a; 4b; 5b; 6c;
7a; 8c; 9b;10b.

**Friday:** 1c; 2c; 3b; 4c; 5a; 6c; 7a;
8a; 9b.

**Saturday:** 1c; 2b; 3c; 4a; 5c; 6b;
7b; 8c; 9a.